INTRODUCTION.

A DETAIL of the circumstances which have oc-
casioned this volume to be added to the long list
of- similar publications, will, it is hoped, form
its best apology ; and conduce, in some degree,
to secure to its Author, the patience and can-
dour of those who may deem themselves entitled
to sit in judgment on his labours. The follow-
ing short Introduction, with some little altera-
tion, is drawn up for the author by a literary
friend.

THOMAS LISTER, whose homely effusions
are now offered to the indulgent inspection of his
numerous supporters, furnishes another instance,
in addition to the many our country has pro-

duced, of the power of the simplest elements of
sound knowledge implanted in the infant breast
and fostered by habits of reflection, to expand
and ripen, as well in the humblest recess of the
vale of poverty as in the abode of competence,
or the mansion of splendour.

Our rustic bard was lured by the charms
of Nature, which luxuriate in his native valley,
and by the trains of contemplation to which ex-
isting events prompted him, to indulge in the
sweet seducements of Poesy, before he had ac-
quired almost any acquaintance with the proud-
est and least perishable of her songs.   Without
having taken the privilege which, to a certain
extent is allowable, of benefiting by the perusal
of other authors,—possessing but a slight know-
ledge of the rules of composition, and still less
of the laws which regulate the standard of taste;
—he has composed, chiefly while pursuing his
daily toils in the open air, many productions
which have found favour amongst those who
know him, and have excited a warm interest in
various parts of the country.   Even criticism,

THE RUSTIC WREATH.

POEMS,

MORAL, DESCRIPTIVE, & MISCELLANEOUS.

—

By *THOMAS LISTER,*

BARNSLEY.

—

LEEDS:

PRINTED FOR THE AUTHOR, BY ANTHONY PICKARD,

CROSS-COURT, TOP OF BRIGGATE;

AND SOLD BY

DARTON AND HARVEY, LONDON.

1834.

TO VISCOUNT MORPETH,

THIS VOLUME OF ORIGINAL POEMS

IS GRATEFULLY INSCRIBED,

BY HIS HUMBLE ADMIRER

AND EARNEST WELL-WISHER,

THE AUTHOR.

ADDRESS TO THE SUBSCRIBERS.

TO you who have so kindly aided me with your free support, I tender my most hearty thanks—the best return which an Author has to bestow. So long as I duly estimate the encouragement you have given to me—so long as I know the value of a few well-timed words, generously spoken in my recommendation,—your unlooked-for kindness will command my gratitude. It only remains for me to express in the usual manner, my ardent hope that your sanction has not been idly and undeservedly bestowed.

To those who, from principle, have avowed some little objection to giving me their aid, lest kindness might prove an injury, I honestly say, that if their motives are good, which they alone can know by examination, I can appreciate their good-will—they are entitled to my sincere esteem: if aught but a kind and Christian spirit has dictated any part of the many admonitions I have received on taking this step, I recommend to them as the most effectual guide to a right judgment, strict inward research and self-amendment.

When I consider that I am submitting the effusions of young inexperience, to the notice of so widely-extended a cir-

cle of readers, amongst whom every shade and extreme of
opinion, and all classes of people may be found; I must de-
clare that every step which I take towards so important a tri-
bunal, is attended with a secret fearfulness and mistrust.   I
am fully aware of the responsibility in which I am placing
myself, and of the many evils to which I am, and shall
be exposed; I am sensible of the great imperfections of my
Work, and I never was more so than I am at present: I
can only request those individuals who, as their minds may be
constituted, will regard the subjects of my choice in a differ-
ent light from myself, to examine the grounds on which my
sentiments rest, and to judge with candour, ere they con-
demn.   I can more readily allow them to say that I have
been mistaken in my views, than that I have knowingly ex-
aggerated a fact or perverted a truth.

The merit of my Poetry I leave altogether as a matter of
opinion; the tendency of it, I trust, is not injurious.   In ac-
cordance with a scriptural admonition, I earnestly wish, in
conclusion, that not only my small talent, but that the en-
dowments and energies of all men, may be more fully and
generally exercised in promoting the growth of every good
principle, in advancing the comfort and moral elevation of
the human race, that so in charity and peace with each
other, we may all combine to fulfil the glorious design of
our Creator.

THOMAS LISTER.

3rd Mo., 1834.

may find an excuse to avert her withering frown
from what she might otherwise have been justified
in considering as an unpruned crudity of style.
This blemish a wider range of study and better
directed taste may ultimately correct.

One of the first subjects which called for
the exercise of his powers, was the departure of
his three brothers to America, during a period of
great commercial depression. Six years he had
suffered to pass by, unimproved, with regard to
mental advancement ;—from the time of leaving
Ackworth School to the attainment of his twen-
tieth year, a dearth of any thing excellent ap-
pears to have reigned in his mind. But re-
flections on the expatriation of his brethren,
gave birth to a Poetical Essay, in which, with
all the ardour of a young politician, he enters
boldly upon concerns of great moment ;—sub-
jects which years of enquiry and debate cannot
fathom, so as to give a satisfactory decision upon
their merits. Since that period, without making
a task of what should be a delight, he has oc-
casionally written other Poems of a varied kind ;

and as all of these, from that diversity, have
shared the approval of some mind that was con-
genial, he has at length been induced to make
them known to a wider circle.

These introductory remarks cannot close
better than by adverting to a circumstance, pro-
minently connected with the subject, which it
becomes the duty of the editor to mention.

Some time after his " warblings wild" had
attracted the notice of his townsmen, and parti-
cularly of James Porter, Esq., of Park-House,
his warmest advocate and weightiest supporter,
a vacancy occurred in the office of Post-Master,
at Barnsley, his native town.   The appointment
of a successor rested with Lord Morpeth, who
had taken great interest in the welfare of this
rising mart of an important branch of British
commerce,—the linen manufacture.   His lord-
ship, remembering the youthful bard who had
been introduced to him during the election for
Yorkshire, generously nominated him to the
office, and was seconded in his choice by the

principal inhabitants of the town. But an insuperable obstacle prevented the fulfilment of his wishes. An oath was then by law required, previous to instalment in a goverment office. Though the contrast between the management of a horse and cart, and the occupation of a profitable situation was greatly in favour of the latter, yet, by Thomas Lister the place could only be filled at the sacrifice of principle. He had been trained up under the eye of honest and revered parents in the principles of the Society of Friends, and the taking of an oath would, in his view, have been a violation of the spirit of a plain command of our Saviour.

His decision, communicated without loss of time to the noble lord, who, in the true spirit of his illustrious ancestors had stretched forth his fostering arms to shelter modest merit, will best appear from a perusal of the following correspondence which took place between them; and which is now published by his lordship's permission, to remain, it is hoped, a record mutually honourable to both.

Barnsley, 12th Mo., 19th, 1832.

To Viscount Morpeth,

      The emotions of astonishment immediately
succeeding the disclosure of this great additional kind-
ness which thou art desirous to confer upon me, are
now wholly absorbed in the deep glow of gratitude.
Thanks, which my rude language cannot declare with
sufficient fervour, arise from my heart unto thee, my
noble and disinterested friend; who, amid the ardu-
ous and trying duties of an exalted station, hast long
silently meditated the welfare of a being so unworthy
as myself.

  Should this providential arrangement succeed, I
hope that I shall be able, through Divine favour, to
occupy the allotted station to the satisfaction of the
public, and to the peace of my own mind,

      Believe me,

      Thy sincerely grateful and obliged friend,

          THOMAS LISTER.

Castle-Howard, Dec. 28th, 1832.

My dear Sir,

      I feel the most sincere regret in announcing
to you that I have just been acquainted by the Post-
Master General, that he cannot appoint any person to

the office of Post-Master, who declines to take the Oath of Office. I am afraid that there is no ground for hoping that you can waive scruples which I must honour, though I cannot enter into them.

I am sorry for the false hopes which must have been raised in you, and which expressed themselves so feelingly in your letter to me; I am still more sorry for my entire want of power to serve a person whom I must continue to regard with increased interest and esteem.

At my request, the Duke of Richmond has returned the Memorial in your favour, and I will direct it to be forwarded by the coach; you may like to preserve it as a gratifying mark of the estimation in which you are held by your fellow-townsmen, and as a record that your general conduct deserved, though your particular principles did not permit you to obtain, success.

I remain,

Your faithful friend,

MORPETH.

Barnsley, 12th Mo., 29th, 1832.

To Viscount Morpeth,

After the perusal of thy consolatory lines, permit me a second time to acknowledge, how deeply

I am bound in obligation to thee, for thy earnest solicitude on my behalf.

On the rejection of the advantageous offer which has been made to me, I could not have expected so cheering a testimony of regard ; neither did I look for so favourable a construction upon, what may be termed, my superstitious scruples—by adherence to which, I have excited considerable displeasure among some of my well-wishers.

No one can more regret than myself the imperative ordinance, which compels me to throw away so great a favour—but this regret cannot overpower my serenity. I would not be here understood as aping the philosopher, or making a boast of my integrity. I dare not lay claim to any merit in the esteem of men, or in the eye of Heaven, from having conscientiously abided by the principles of my forefathers ;—yet I am convinced, that a cool deviation from what I believe to be a positive duty, would have embittered every sensation of delight, and every comfort, which brightening fortune might have placed in my power.

I am very desirous to remove the painful impressions which thy kind epistle declares, are felt on my account. I am favoured to bear resignedly this stroke of disappointment. Knowing the fading nature of all earthly prospects, I suffered not my hopes to rise above my control. Sufficient time has been allowed me to contemplate a reverse; in consequence I am not so deeply depressed in spirits, now that an unforeseen obstacle has frustrated the accomplishment of a desirable object.

Ashamed that I have been the unhappy cause of trouble and·anxiety to many,—warmly sensible of the generous exertions which have been made to promote my welfare,—and trusting that I may never forfeit the good opinion which is too lavishly entertained of me,

I have the honour to subscribe myself,

Thy obliged friend,

THOMAS LISTER.

CONTENTS.

                                                   Page.

ON THE CULTIVATION OF THE INTELLECTUAL FA-
CULTIES, ... xix.

THE RUSTIC REASONERS, ... 1
ANSELLA, ... 12
THE YORKSHIRE HIRINGS, ... 23
THE HOME-EXPELLED BRITONS, ... 40
GENERAL MEETING AT ACKWORTH SCHOOL, ... 50
EYEING-WOOD FIELDS, ... 59
GREENFIELD HILLS, ... 64
IRISH WANDERER, ... 68
TRIUMPH OF PURE LOVE OVER DIFFICULTY, ... 73
REFLECTIONS, ... 82
TRIBUTE OF CONSOLATION, ... 91
WRECK OF THE ROTHSAY-CASTLE, ... 97
WAIL OF THE PROFLIGATE, ... 101
POLAND'S LAST STRUGGLE, ... 108

	Page.
TRUE FRIENDSHIP,	111
ODE TO HUMANITY,	113
THE HAPPY SURPRISE,	117
A GLANCE AT STUDLEY AND HACKFALL,	121
FAREWELL TO PINDER OAKS,	129
WELCOME TO A GOLDEN GIFT,	132
TO AN EARLY FRIEND ON A LONG SEPARATION,	137
TRIBUTE TO THE GENIUS OF BURNS,	141
ON THE LOSS OF A PROMISING YOUTH,	144
TO M——,	146
DAVID'S LAMENTATION,	149
REPROOF OF A WORLDLY SPIRIT, (ECCLES. v.)	151
HONEY WELL,	154
MORNING CONTEMPLATIONS,	156
ON THE OBSERVATORY AT MONK-BRETTON, NEAR BARNSLEY,	161
ON ARRIVING AT MANHOOD,	165
ON THE DEATH OF DR. OXLEY,	174
A PRAYER,	176
THE EMIGRANT MOTHER TO HER FIRST-BORN,	180
SUBSCRIBERS' NAMES,	185

ON THE CULTIVATION OF THE IN-TELLECTUAL FACULTIES.

(WRITTEN FOR AN ESSAY MEETING.)

IN this age of public discussion, and private enquiry, when all subjects interesting to human reason, and dear to the feelings of our nature, are brought before our eyes in every variety of form, distinguished by every shade of ability,—whether the laboured work of the deep-thoughted philosopher or the momentary effusion of the humble essay writer;—at this remarkable period, teeming with information, a further excitement given to the desire for intellectual improvement, already so powerfully manifested, may be deemed uncalled-for and unnecessary.

But, where knowledge is infused, and faculties are awakened in a mind, which before was uninformed and in a great measure inactive, it naturally follows that such a mind, happily aroused from an inglorious repose, will be actuated by a generous impulse to communicate to others the new-found sources of wonder

and delight. Where an Essay, ushered into being un-
der circumstances like these, eventually fails to gain
the merit of a well-arranged, well-finished composi-
tion, many will charitably withhold censure, and some
will even be disposed to admire that enthusiasm which
impels the young aspirant to aim at an important re-
sult, which his limited powers do not permit him to
reach.

Nothing new is here presented to the reader. The
object of this article is to enforce, by repetition in a
compressed manner, lessons of wisdom which must
have been often expressed before, by some of those
deep thinkers, and accurate reasoners, whose well-
read volumes proclaim the value of their authors.

When a disposition to cultivate the nobler endow-
ments of our race is manifested, and especially by
young people, no impediment should be allowed to
to check the way of improvement;—but, on the con-
trary, every care should be taken to foster, those de-
sires, where mental enjoyments are preferred to the
mere pleasures of sense, by all, who either from the
force of example, or the influence of authority, can
exercise a direct control in the formation of cha-
racter.

This disposition, under the control of sound rea-

son, wandering not beyond a proper limit, nor pursu-
ing aught which may prejudice interests of higher mo-
ment, has often been the means of securing to its pos-
sessor, sources of the purest delight,—has often been
instrumental in counteracting or alleviating, many of
the bitter evils which so blightingly assail the wander-
ers of a changeful scene.

Who, that is conscious of the dignity of man,
above the subordinate creation;—who, that feelingly
knows the value of that unlimited mind which a bene-
ficent Creator has conferred upon him, can bear with
patience the presence of that individual, however
comely in person and goodly in array, who mingles
unblushingly amongst his species, but scarcely dis-
plays more intelligence than the grazing tenants of
the field? What different feelings do they excite in
our minds, who have not lived altogether unprofita-
bly, nor despised the distinguishing prerogative which
elevates man above the irrational world? In their
sweet hours of leisure, they have laudably endeavoured
to store up treasures in the capacious chambers of the
soul, which will not be disturbed in the rude visita-
tions of calamity, nor rifled amidst all the changes of
an uncertain state. They have it in their power to
make themselves agreeably instructive whilst sitting
in "sweet society," exchanging mutual advantages
with their fellow beings. With them frivolity will

be discarded, and slander shut out.   The conversation
need not flow heavily, nor the hours move wearily.

When this privilege of seeking delight in the com-
pany of others is denied to them, they have still valu-
able resources of which the dull world knows nothing.
In every situation they can find some agreeable object,
some instructive companion, as their genius or natural
disposition may lead them.   The glories of Nature
and the triumphs of art, are laid open for their inspec-
tion.   In the closet, their bosom friends are the elo-
quent and the wise, of all times.

If they walk beyond the precincts of bustling life,
how abundant the tranquil joys which await them!
The earth, our present abode,—its diversified figure
and grand conformation,—the rich treasures it contains
—the plants and verdure which crown its surface,
from the storm-defying king of the forest, to the mo-
dest floweret that smiles beneath the hedge-row—the
animals, various in their forms as different in their
habits, which dwell on the ground or sport in the rest-
less flood, and the active beings which joy in a lighter
element, making with ease their path in the air, and
stooping only to earth to appease their wants and in-
dulge their pleasures ;—these creations of an intelligent,
all-ruling Mind, revealed without restraint to the gaze
of his humblest children, invite to calm and pleasing

investigation. At one view, as a whole they irresistibly awaken a general admiration, while each has attractions of its own kind, claims individual attention, and yields to the votary of research its own peculiar reward.

There are still nobler studies, furnished by the experience and learning of past ages, the observations of the present time, and the sure revelation of God:— the study of promoting as far as our power enables us to do so, the comfort and happiness of our fellow-beings—and the higher study of learning the will of our Heavenly Ruler, and obeying its injunctions with zeal and sincerity.

To these all other things must be subservient. On these all-involving objects, the designs of Omnipotence centre: for this end the powers of thought and of reason were conferred upon man, and by the right employment of these gifts will man secure the eternal triumph of the mind.

T. L.

POEMS.

THE RUSTIC REASONERS;

A SUPPOSED CONVERSATION BETWEEN TWO SWAINS, TA-
KING PLACE IN THE GARRET OF AN OLD FARM-HOUSE.
THE TIME IS DAY-BREAK IN SUMMER. NEITHER
THEY NOR THEIR SENTIMENTS ARE ALTOGETHER
IMAGINARY. ONE, WHO IS MORE POLISHED AND BET-
TER INFORMED THAN THE OTHER, I CALL TOM—HIS
DULL COMPANION, JOE.

TOM.

WAKE! slumbering mortal, from thy dull repose,
Light, o'er the gloom, her first faint mantle throws,
While through each pane and chink her arrows dart,
She bids soft sleep and airy dreams depart;

B

The feather'd choir, to hail the rising morn,
Their anthems pour from every blossom'd thorn,
Loud, from his perch, shrill-throated Chanticleer
Proclaims, with joy, the orb of day is near:
Let us, like them, the bonds of sleep disdain,
And cheerful toil in bright Aurora's train.

JOE.

Tormenting youth, to pinch and pull me thus,
Let go my arm,—why make this needless fuss
To rouse me, from my peaceful sleep, so soon?
Thy fancied sun will only prove the moon;
That voice of birds is but the nightingale's,
Whose pleasing note through night's dull reign pre-
    vails:
Think not to rise at this untimely hour,
But yield once more to slumber's lingering power.

TOM.

Forbear such nonsense,—are my senses fled,
Or, like thy own, by stupid error led?
Dost thou suppose I cannot judge aright,
Betwixt the moonbeam and the sun's glad light?—
The notes of Philomela, and the song
Of daylight birds, the neighbouring trees among?

That morn is near, all sounds, all objects show,
But, who so dull, as they who will not know?
Lo! there the sun-saluting lark upsprings,
And warbles blithe, while pois'd on steady wings;
The blackbird whistles in the garden-bush,
In yonder wood I hear the mellow thrush,
Fly-chasing swallows try their fleetest speed,
And, twittering 'neath the eaves, their nestlings
    feed;
The linnet swells its simple notes around,
With the full chorus fields and groves resound :—
To song or toil, each self-taught power 's applied,
Some, homes construct,—some, nourishment pro-
    vide,
By instinct led, a never-erring guide;
They, with the bees, now humming forth below,
Of art and skill, the fairest emblems show.

JOE.

Unless it be the humming, minstrel art,
To thee their tasks no lesson will impart;
Though not the fruits of thy own plodding care,
While aught is left, thou wilt not miss thy share;
But, in the labours which they daily ply,
To imitate them thou wilt never try.

TOM.

If thou incline to be severely smart,
Take care thy wit is polish'd well by art;
Although 't is right for thee to speak thy mind,
Thou canst not steer against a baffling wind;
My station here, is higher than thy own,
Hence, some degree of deference should be shown,—
Thy words assail thyself as well as me,
Since thou and labour seldom long agree;
At meals, too, thou thy part dost freely play,
Whilst I enjoy them in a moderate way:
In valued books, and observation made,
I trust to guides that seldom have betray'd;
These, while they point true pleasures to my sight,
From folly, sloth, intemperance, urge my flight,
Fair Nature's order show, and Nature's law,
And bid me thence the choicest precepts draw,
With warm, devout sensations fill my mind,
And prompt to good pursuits—though far I lag
      behind.

JOE.

In learned strain I would not soar so high,
For fear of tumbling when I fain would fly;

Few stores of science overload my brain,
My rules of life from humbler source I gain ;
'T is well, in these strange times, I earn my bread,
And not with mazy studies turn my head :
To eat, drink, rest,—life's comforts to enjoy,
Are all the objects that my cares employ ;
Whereas, thy precepts, when to trial brought,
Are not so smooth in practice as in thought.
Though praising temperance, and early hours,
I 'm apt to think thy rules exceed thy powers ;
In circles wont to hear the minstrel's lays,
No doubt good cheer rewards, as well as praise,—
Returning, lighted by the stars or moon,
Thy hour of rest is late, or rather, soon ;
To early rising thou art seldom prone,
Unless when mov'd by fancies of thy own.
Thus, more and more, I prove that maxim true,
Fine words are plenteous, but good actions few,
Since thou, with lore and moral precepts bless'd,
Art but an erring creature like the rest.

TOM.

Without a fault was never mortal found.
Frailties, alas ! the best of men surround ;

In every breast some master-passion reigns,
Which heaven-entrusted reason scarce restrains:
By nature prone to evil, from his birth
Dark imperfection brands the child of earth;
Imperfect culture mars the noblest seed,
Examples vile from paths of virtue lead,—
Habits, contracted in life's earlier stage,
Or good or ill, grow more confirm'd by age;
But few indeed can curb each wayward will,
And truly virtuous minds are fewer still:
Oh! how should I, though train'd with fondest care,
Escape the ills which all are doom'd to bear?
I bound along, a fickle, vagrant child,
O'er rude, eccentric paths,—unfetter'd, wild;
Yet, in my wildest flights, by passion drawn,
Some virtuous gleams around me faintly dawn;
E'en where the festive cup is gaily quaff'd,
I shun the sensualist's degrading draught,—
Though lingering oft amid these scenes of joy,
I mark how soon voluptuous pleasures cloy,
The vile-drugg'd cup I hence forbear to taste,
Nor dare in mental sloth my moments waste;
The ways of erring life are there display'd
In all their strange degrees of light and shade;
I learn, while in these devious tracks I run,
To prize all virtue more,—all vice to shun,

Since vice o'er every joy extends a gloom,
While virtue smiles in ever-during bloom.
Though coarse my manners, and my phrase uncouth,
My conduct shadow'd by the faults of youth,
Of culture bare,—though small my mental skill
To mount, triumphant, learning's arduous hill,—
Though but a rude foundation here is laid,
Yet much is gain'd from heavenly Wisdom's aid ;
As art and skill on some weak shatter'd pile,
Bid grace and splendour, renovated, smile—
So she reforms each frail, degenerate mind,
And they who Wisdom seek, will surely find ;—
As she to aid, were I to toil as free,
What noble triumphs would remain for me :
Imperial Rome, who once her flag unfurl'd,
The awful mistress of a subject world,—
Whose fame, through ages, has so proudly blaz'd,
Was not by instantaneous effort, rais'd ;
Without unwearied toil, no great design
E'er reach'd success, nor with neglect will mine.
If one by one my faults I cast aside,
And let their place with virtues be supplied,
Unlike too many of the preaching race,
My words and deeds will keep an equal pace ;
I then may hope, while Wisdom sways my pen,
In Truth's high cause to serve my fellow-men,—

For Heaven ordains, that mortals here below
Should well their talents and their gifts bestow ;
Within each breast one sacred impulse feel,
To toil for general, as for private, weal ;
And humbly strive, in their allotted hour,
To cherish good, as they are bless'd with power.
But oh ! what sons of pamper'd ease abound,
Who merely live as cumberers of the ground,—
Pursue ambition, pleasure, folly, gain,
Nor care to soothe a fellow-mortal's pain ;
Nor Heaven's kind gifts, in shedding bounty, use,
Like flowing fountains, or refreshing dews :
And many are there of the toiling race,
Whom ignorance holds within her dull embrace,
Who, while they swell some great employer's store,
See famine, watching at their friendless door ;
E'en here will legal rapine boldly glide,
Despoiling bees, that drones may be supplied :
They, wanting knowledge, are bereft of power,
To ward off harpies, who their stores devour :
But less, this abject spirit, we survey,
Where wisdom spreads her intellectual ray ;
For as she lifts her sacred standard, high,
Oppression, fraud, and crouching ignorance fly ;
While freedom's flames the human breast inspire,
Igniting swiftly like electric fire ;

Intolerance strives to hold her seat in vain,
Wide rends th' intriguing snare, and shivering falls
    the chain.
But why should I my words so idly throw
On one, who will not half their purport know ;
On aid like thine, should friends of Truth depend,
Their cause, *howe'er* advanc'd, would backward tend,
Regeneration's course, impeded, stay,
And freedom's fires, in hopeless gloom decay :
For, while I freely pour my treasur'd store,
Thou merely answer'st with a nod or snore ;
I might as well address a stone, or tree,
The god of sleep yields far more charms for thee.

JOE.

No ; I have heard thee well ; thy doctrine 's true,
Well worth the hearing and regarding too ;
And while conviction I most strongly feel,
To prize it duly, I will show my zeal :
Now, but once more, I'll turn my drowsy head,
And then, without a murmur, quit my bed.

TOM.

Stay as thou wilt, indulge thy lethargy,
Thy wavering spirit shall not influence me ;

I rise at once, and through the window peep,
The sun is flaming o'er the eastern steep,
The shades of night are fled—and roof, and spire,
Above the town, seem tipp'd with solar fire ;
While morn her robes in fairy-beauty weaves,
O'er dew-drench'd fields and shadow-blending leaves,
His warmth, descending on the fertile earth,
Bids nature smile, and wakes the embryo birth :
The healing plant, the variegated flower,
The tender herbage, and the budding bower,
Confess his mighty vivifying ray,
And joyful anthems greet the coming day ;
While harvest, smiling, crown'd with shooting grain,
Holds forth her brightest hopes to cheer the swain.
On all sides, labourers to their toil repair,
None now will sleep, but those devoid of care ;
The kine, upon the bare-worn pasture stand,
Or, ruminating, wait the milker's hand ;
There browse the steeds the juicy morsel choice ;
Their ears erecting at the driver's voice ;
And in their looks a strong desire I read
Before their toil on ampler stores to feed ;
Fresh grass I'll mow, their craving to allay,
While on the glebe the moistening dew-drops stay.
Hark ! now the clamorous inmates of the sty,
In chorus shrill, exalt their morning cry ;

The ducks are waddling round in quest of food,
And fierce the hen conducts her tender brood ;
Led by their strutting chief, the poultry train,
Around the door, demand the welcome grain :
I go, each eager appetite to still,
For these must feed, let times be good or ill.
Some by their milk or toil maintain me now,
Upon the rest my cares I must bestow,
That when they fall beneath the stern decree,
As now I nourish them, so they may nourish me.

ANSELLA.*

I.

ASSIST my trembling lyre, O mournful muse!
  Come, in thy robe of deepest gloom array'd!
While streams of pity flow, like kindly dews,
  Let no light airs the solemn theme pervade;
In this sad tale of death, and flood, and fire,
Breathe deeply-moving words, and fervent thoughts
    inspire.

---

* The amiable subject of this poem, ANSELLA BOAG, was on her return from a visit paid to her brothers in Carolina—in company with one of those brothers and several eminent individuals. A violent storm came on, attended with thunder and lightning. The noble ship was struck by the electric fluid and consumed to the water's edge, and the crew and passengers in the boats braved the fury of the combined elements. This young lady, after displaying great firmness and piety, expired in the arms of her brother. The melancholy catastrophe occurred a few years since.

II.

The drifting clouds, along the murky sky
  In boding aspect overhung the main,
Whose waters dash'd with loud and angry cry,
  Sunk in deep vales, and proudly heav'd again;
·The rising winds with blustering fury howl'd,
Defiance breathing loud, by mortals uncontroll'd.

III.

A ship then plough'd the darkly swelling wave,
  From lovely Charleston to Britannia bound,
Her captain gallant and her seamen brave,
  Alert and vigorous at their station found;
A worthy train her splendid cabin bore,
By various motives led, to Albion's pleasant shore.

IV.

Scarce had the land slow faded from the eye, '
  Ere heavy squalls above, tremendous broke;
In horror frown'd the wild and lurid sky,
  And swelling seas beat high with furious stroke,
While through th' aërial vault, in dread presage,
The thunder bellow'd loud, the lightning spent its rage.

V.

Chang'd were the looks—deep-mov'd the hearts of all;
  Where joy and ardour rul'd the last glad hour,
Now sad depression cast a gloomy pall,
  And terror wak'd its all-infecting power ;
Yet still, at duty's post, a steadfast slave
The seaman dauntless toil'd, his valued charge to
    save.

VI.

Thus, through the black impending gloom,—they
    steer,
  Now glimmering flash the skies—now darkly
    frown,—
At length, the lightning, in its wild career,
  Lur'd by the bark, came fiercely streaming
    down ;
Soon, the deep hold, fraught with electric fire,
Belch'd cloudy volumes forth, with suffocating ire.

VII.

The flaming ruin glided swift along ;
  Each nervous sinew was in vain applied

To quell its force, so fearful and so strong ;—
    The boats were launch'd upon the angry tide,—
Their stores resign'd, at nature's weightier call ;
Life—precious life, the cry—all other cares were
    small.

VIII.

So, when a conquering host, with haughty tread,
    O'erwhelming, drench a smiling land with blood,
And wasting fire, and heavy ruin spread,—
    What, though a time their fury be withstood,
The natives fly, too weak their march to stay,
Flocks, herds, and stores remain, to hostile rage a
    prey !

IX.

'T is midnight now,—a dread appalling hour !
    Yet here as light as is the brightest day ;
The conflagration's still augmenting power,
    Forc'd through the masts and shrouds its head-
    long way,
And bursting, roaring with insatiate pride,
Annihilated all, till vanquish'd by the tide.

X.

Above, no moon diffus'd her friendly glow,
  But vivid lightning shot a tenfold glare,
No stars were mirror'd in the deep below,—
  Fire sheets, red glancing, were reflected there,
While the mad waves, as they, resounding, roll'd,
Rear'd, in terrific pomp, their crests like molten gold.

XI.

With rumbling peals did Heaven's vast arch rebound ;
  Man shook as though he heard his awful knell ;
The tempest howl'd in sullen wrath around,
  And o'er their heads dark bursting torrents fell :
What perils, unforeseen, were theirs to brave ;
Who toss'd in open boats, on the devouring wave.

XII.

But how can my weak hand essay to paint,
  The woes and dangers of this dismal night,
To image which all hues would prove but faint,
  Where shone no ray of mild relieving light ?
Hope fled afar, while horror brooded there,
Keen rending anguish smote, and gloomy-brow'd
    despair.

XIII.

How seldom thinks the sensual child of ease,
　Who fruitless wastes the swift-revolving day,
Of storms, of hardships, and of boisterous seas,
　Strewing with pain and death the seaman's way,—
What sympathy awaits the daring toil,
Which wins his choicest stores from every clime and
　　soil ?

XIV.

Above the rest, one precious being drew
　Most deep concern,—a sweet, endearing maid ;
No louring danger could her heart subdue,—
　For, while the flames with quenchless fury spread,
(Serene and firm, no slave to shrinking fear,)
She stimulated all, throughout their toil severe.

XV.

Thou, lov'd Ansella, wert a vernal flower,
　Expanding to the sun rich opening charms ;
Nor beauty only, virtue was thy dower,
　And sweet affection that progressive warms :
A bright example to the youthful race,
In thee refinement shone, with mild, engaging grace.

XVI.

Thou, plac'd beneath a kind protector's care,
  Far from this isle didst brave the Atlantic's
    roar;
Two brothers dear breath'd the free Western air,
  Where Charleston smiles on Carolina's shore;
Their home inviting, mov'd thy young desire
To prove the hallow'd joys which kindred souls
    inspire.

XVII.

Thrice the fair earth resign'd her flowery grace,
  And thrice the glorious sun of Summer shone,
Ere thou didst leave the hospitable race;
  Such powerful motives thy compliance won,
Still to prolong a welcome stay with these,
Where solid pleasures charm'd, civility and ease.

XVIII.

The people shar'd thy love, the land as well,
  Yet was another land to thee more dear;
And, in thy breast, did lively transports swell,
  When fancy bade home's sweeter scenes appear:

Hoping to smile with all so cherish'd there,
How little didst thou deem that none this joy might
    share !

XIX.

Such was the maid, who, in this cheerless hour,
    The mingling wrath of storm and sea withstood ;
But soon she languish'd like a slender flower,
    That bows its head beneath the pouring flood :
A firm support this gentle one possess'd,
Her brother fondly sooth'd, and clasp'd her to his
    breast.

XX.

Though calm her mind beneath this lot severe,
    Her tender frame could not endure the stroke ;
And how could she this dreadful trial bear,
    Which harass'd men, unshrinking as the oak ?
For kindly guarded had her nurture been,
Beneath maternal care, amid each peaceful scene.

XXI.

On her the lightning, and the thunder's peal,
    So terrible to some—no fears impress'd ;

No peace-impairing anguish did she feel,
   No guilty thoughts were harbour'd in her breast:
This truth how sure, a heart unstain'd by vice,
Yields, e'en in death's dark hour, the calm of Paradise.

XXII.

Though she had cherish'd lively hope before,
   To see her kindred, friends, and native land,—
Yet did she not this blighting stroke deplore,
   But bow'd, submissive, to the chastening hand,—
Firm trusting, through divine, redeeming grace,
To find, in brighter worlds, a glorious resting-place.

XXIII.

As o'er her cheeks, which bloom'd of late so fair,
   The rose-blush wasting, snowy paleness spread;
As sunk her frame, unmeet such load to bear,
   Before her calm and gentle spirit fled,—
Her lips implor'd of Heaven, in fervent prayer,
To guard her suffering friends, with kind sustaining care.

XXIV.

As the sweet babe, upon its mother's breast,
   Lock'd in the warm embrace, soft slumbering lies,

So, in her brother's arms, she sunk to rest,—
  His gentle hand for ever clos'd her eyes ;
All hearts were sad, and mute was every tongue,
As o'er her lovely form the storm-beat mourners
    hung.

XXV.

Is there a bosom whence no sigh would rise,
  O'er scenes like this,—or eye that would not
    weep ?
If so, let such the kindlier feeling prize,
  Which warm'd these ill-starr'd wanderers of the
    deep ;
Who, though a thousand dangers roll'd around,
Perform'd her funeral rites, with zeal and awe pro-
    found.

XXVI.

That her fair body thus was thrown to feed
  The watery brood, may move a thought of glóom ;
Yet dire necessity for this must plead,
  Distressful sequel of a sadder doom :
How oft the gloomy, unreposing wave,
Oblivious shroud! hath wrapp'd the beauteous and
    the brave.

XXVII.

Her dying prayer, that Heaven might aid the rest,
   Rose not to Mercy's gracious throne in vain;
A welcome sail their wearied vision bless'd,
   Oh! kind relief, to deep distress and pain;
Their grateful feelings need no tongue to tell,
For all, with mind endued, their state may image well.

XXVIII.

Though freed from peril and soul-withering fear,
   A something wanting, their dejection told;
To them, than gold or orient pearls more dear,
   This richest treasure in the dark waves roll'd;
For her a Mother, Sisters, Brethren, weep,
And friendly hearts lament, in tribulation deep.

XXIX.

And oft, where dark Atlantic waters spread,
   Wide, wide afar, will restless memory roam;
Long pensive wail the wave-toss'd, urnless dead,
   Who, in these depths, hath found a final home,
When fire-fraught storms above wild threatening roll,
Sad tears will fall afresh—new darkness veil the soul!

THE YORKSHIRE HIRINGS.

BLEAK wintry days were nearing fast,
Through half-stripp'd woodlands roar'd the blast,
The brown leaves whirl'd in sportive round,
Or, sere and wither'd, strew'd the ground ;
No flowerets, tipp'd with sparkling dew,
On sunny bank or meadow grew,—
No songster chaunted from the thorn,—
No blithe-ton'd milkmaid charm'd the morn :
The kine, by night, in straw-roof'd shed,
On hay or juicy turnips fed ;
No steeds on naked pastures brows'd,
But champ'd their fodder, snugly hous'd :
O'er fields, late deck'd with smiling corn,
The hunter rode, while twang'd the horn ;
The sportsman, with relentless aim,
Spread death amongst the flying game ;
The patient swains, with ceaseless care,
For future crops the soil prepare,
In fondest hope the well-till'd earth
Might bless them with her richest birth.

One morning, in that season chill,
(Which makes dull spirits gloomier still,)
Though light her earliest streaks display'd,
No gorgeous tints the East array'd ;
As though to greet men's gaze, too proud,
The sun rose, veil'd in dismal shroud,
When, plodding on a lonely lane,
Were seen a motley rustic train ;
The whole, trimm'd neatly in their best,
Spoke this a day of welcome rest :
These worthy children of the soil,
Had bid a short adieu to toil,—
Brute, slave, and man, alike must play,
For 't is the annual Hiring-Day :
To gain employ were some intent,
A few on pleasure's errand bent,—
To guide rash youth, grey wisdom went.

A simply clad, time-honour'd man,
In steady order led the van ;
Though life's brief sand was sinking low,
Yet dignity sat on his brow :
The sinew large, and bony limb,
Show'd vigour once had dwelt with him,
His rugged hand most truly told,
A life in usefulness " grown old ;"

That hand had been the steadfast friend,
On which he could the most depend,—
Hence, he would never bow, to please
The pamper'd sons of lordly ease;
For he, to Nature's purpose true,
Enrich'd the soil whereon he grew;
Though plenty never swell'd his store,
He found content, and sought no more:
His sons and daughters, blooming round,
Long smil'd upon their native ground,
And, branching from the parent tree,
Like healthy blossoms, flourish'd free.
One son, beside his buxom dame,
A man of stout and hardy frame,
Walk'd next, with firm, resounding stride,
Rejoicing in his manhood's pride:
From one of those great lords of land,
Who, o'er wide regions stretch the hand,
A farm he held, of scanty bound,
Where toil a bare subsistence found;
His sons, advancing fast to men,
Two sturdy youths, were with him then,
A daughter staid in charge at home,
With prattling bairns too small to come:
Their cot the honour'd grandsire grac'd,
While life declin'd with gentle waste;

C

Experience prov'd a rich resource,
When ruder powers had lost their force ;
Although a wealthier son liv'd near,
He chose to end his labours here.
When some to him that subject broke,
Thus native independence spoke,—
" While sailing on life's troubled stream,
" The gifts of fortune various teem,
" A few to wealth and power are born,
" While many smart from penury's thorn ;
" And some, who rudest labours share,
" Can find both joy and comfort there ;
" Some, lifted from the lowly train,
" View old connections with disdain,—
" Though worldly treasure they possess
" Alone, it yields not happiness ;
" The joy we more than all should prize,
" A clean and honest heart supplies:
" My son, whom Heaven hath bless'd with gold,
" May yet some kindred feelings hold,
" But I shall fill my quiet grave,
" Ere I from him a bounty crave."

The tale resume—thus far digress'd,
These brief remarks will sketch the rest ;

Their orphan niece, Susannah, fair,
Tripp'd light behind the honest pair ;
Lov'd scenes she left, and bosoms kind,
Another home—less dear—to find ;
Her playful eye and artless mien,
Declar'd that brilliant age, eighteen ;
Dark curls those cheeks did sweetly shade,
Where joy with rosy beauty play'd.
A comely youth, robust, and tall,
Bid love's kind glance on Susan fall ;
And, as a mutual fervour burn'd,
His smile she bashfully return'd,—
First kindled at a country feast,
The flame had ever since increas'd :
On love's light wing he now had flown,
To guard his dearest to the town.
There was, besides, a thoughtless rake,
Whose heart no warning voice could shake,—
A roving lad, to peace a foe,
His friends' regret—his parents' woe,
Who never long to labour bent,
And soon his little earnings spent.
Of vigorous lad, and sprightly lass,
Who form'd the rest, no more I class,—
Still, as they mov'd, their numbers swell'd,
As labour now her pastime held ;

No rain,—for rain began to fall,—
Their steps could check, or hearts appal ;
Each youth his smock around him roll'd,
With swinging gait advancing bold,—
Each maid, just rais'd her flouncing skirt,
And tripp'd, defying wet and dirt ;
The old man crack'd his liveliest jest,
And oft his moral rules impress'd,—
Each farm, and field, that came to view,
The owner and the soil he knew,
And told his tales, (oft told before,)
Of what had there occurr'd of yore,
When youthful blood inspir'd his veins,
And he was hail'd the first of swains.

The high-road won, so smooth and strong,
With brisker step they trudg'd along ;
A band of sharpers, by the way,
Were plotting how to wile their prey,
And soon an artful plan they try,
To catch the unsuspecting eye ;
The veteran bid his charge beware,
Of venturing near the dangerous snare,
Pass'd by the gang, who, muttering, swore,
Then gave this monitory lore,—

" We need to walk with wakeful eyes,
" In every path a danger lies ;
" What various schemes the vile employ,
" To rob us of a fleeting toy ;
" What worthless vermin mar the soil,
" Who seek to live on others' toil ;—
" What some acquire, by sweat and pain,
" By force, or cunning, these obtain—
" And widely doth this spirit reign—
" Far greater, than these outcasts vile,
" By wrong uphold a princely style."

The lively, bustling town, they gain,
Whose wonders greet the simple train ;
Sights, 'passing all they ever saw,
Loud praise from young admirers draw ;
Here, showmen's booths present to view
Fine pictures, not to nature true,
On rows of stalls, are gaily spread,
Toys, trinkets, tape, and gingerbread,—
All, smarten'd up in decent pride,
The rustics flock from every side,
While dialects, of various twàng,
Are heard in homely, brief harangue ;—
Loud laughter roars, when, in the street,
Two old acquaintance chance to meet :

With eager, and unbidden glee,
One bawls—" Ae, Bess lass, is that thee ;
" Ha' ar' ta yet ?—ha' gets ta on ?"
" O, hearty lass—and hae's yoar John ?
" An' hae dus Sal an' Dolly do ?"
—" All weel, an' they're coom hither too."
The house, at times like these, so dear,
Invites them to inspiring beer,
In comfort set, and happy ease,
They relish well their bread and cheese ;
A favourite place our rustics sought,
Where welcome kind was freely bought,
Around a joyful, blazing fire,
They dried their dripping-wet attire,
Concluding there at eve to meet,
They took their station in the street.

A martial train paraded round,
(Whose music peal'd with clangorous sound,)
With young recruits, for whom the tear,
By parting friends, was shed sincere :
Though many gaz'd with strange delight,
There were, who shunn'd the odious sight,
To whose now sad, excited thought,
A kinsman's tragic doom it brought ;

This was poor Susan's ill-starr'd sire,
Who, burning wild with valour's fire,
(And not from want, for labourers then
Were amply paid, contented men,)
Forsook his sad, despairing bride,
To be the slave of power and pride ;
He prov'd his dreams of glory vain,
On Salamanca's bloody plain.

The sun, burst from his cloudy veil,
Gave brighter grace to features hale,
And whisper'd hopes of evening mild,
To those whose early walk was wild.
From youths and maidens, throng'd in rows,
Employers now their servants chose ;
Each youth prepares this answer true,
To " Na, my lad, what can ta deu ?"
While vacant eyes they downward fix,
And scrape the pebbles with their sticks,—
" Wha, aw can plew the streitest furra,
" An so', an' mo', an' team, an' 'arra,
" As weel as ony man a't spot,—
" An' good 's the caricter aw've got:
The girls, to each enquiring dame,
Their merits testified the same,—

" Well, I can wash, an' bake, an' brew,

" An' milk, an' manage t' dairy teu."

The numbers hir'd were rather small,

And low the binding terms with all ;

A dame, on modest Sue, had cast

A glance, which almost through her pass'd,

And was about to speak a word,

When interrupted by a third ;

For Sue was beckon'd to a friend,

Who this advice did freely lend,—

" If yo' wi' her agreement make,

" The bond you'll shortly want to braak ;

" I kno' her weel—a screwing jade,

" Who finds a faut, where noan is made ;"

At this, the matron they forsook,

Who threw on both a scowling look.

But soon the youth who priz'd her best,

His charming Susan thus address'd,—

" Since thou hast got no place to-day,

" Let me thy Hiring-penny pay,

" At thy ill-speed, I somehow feel

" Delight, not easy to conceal ;

" For, if divided, how forlorn

" Thy lost endearments I should mourn ;

" As thou alone my pain could'st ease,
" And, in my weariest moments, please ;
" Who wak'd, in my fond breast, a store
" Of joys I never knew before.
Then soft replied the maiden dear,
" Though all is sweet, while thou art near,
" Yet, when from service I am free,
" What home of comfort waits for me ;
" My uncle, he is free and kind,
" But has enough his own to mind."
" Then, hear me, Susan, cried the youth,
" Thou wilt not, canst not, doubt my truth,—
" Our courtship now has lasted long,
" The tie that binds our hearts is strong,
" With thee I never could repine,
" Whatever sky's above—be mine :
" For not chill, daunting poverty
" Shall quench the flame of love in me ;
" A fair employ I now possess,
" If small my wage, my cost is less ;
" Although my savings are but bare,
" My scanty all with thee I'll share ;
" And we, by dearest union bless'd,
" Must brave all weathers like the rest."
The yielding maid held down her head,
To hide the streaks of deeper red ;

Then, lightly by her lover's side,
To view the scenes of wonder, hied.

For now, the hiring-business done,
Intent to close the day with fun,
In various ways the rustics sped,
By pleasure and by fancy led :
Some, first the splendid shows survey,
With painted canvass waving gay,—
These, creatures hold from every land,—
Those, pantomime, or sleight of hand ;
But spite of music, lies, and din,
More gaze without, than enter in.
Some to the shops and stalls repair,
To spend what trifle they can spare,
Or, round the ballad-mongers crowd,
Who chaunt their jingling strains aloud ;
But far the greater number swarm,
To reeking tavern, dry and warm,
And there, in draughts of cordial brown,
Both sense of thirst and trouble drown.

The sun now bade our clime farewell,
And swift the gathering shadows fell,—
The night-clouds, as they blackening roll'd,
Of distant home the sober told.

The group I oft have nam'd before,
All duly met—with many more ;
'Yet then, to quit the cheerful fire,
Not one express'd a strong desire :
Perhaps the thought had struck their brain,
They might not all meet thus again,—
From giving mirth a loosen'd string
But once a year—no harm might spring :—
The strong ale first the grandsire cheers,
A mark of deference to his years,—
His worthy son partook the same,
And pass'd it over to his dame—
The youths drank free,—e'en each sweet lass,
Press'd warmly, sipp'd her spirit-glass.
As high the mounting potion flew,
Her mantle, Joy around them threw ;
Each heart felt more and more unstrung,
And looser grew each rattling tongue :
Now, in a room, which o'er them lay,
A fiddler blithe began to play ;
As chargers at the trumpet's sound
Erect their ears and paw the ground,
Some rise responsive to the string,
And wild their limbs around them fling,
And caper on the floor amain,
Then, out of breath, sit down again ;

But some run bouncing up the stairs,
Where lads and lasses, rang'd in pairs,
Dance jocund to the sprightly tone,
While floor, and ceiling, shake and groan.
'Mong those below, who jovial sat,
With pipe, and glass, in mingled chat,
Though now they laugh, and now they sing,
The seeds of strife began to spring ;
With heated brain, and reeling pate,
Two youths engag'd in loud debate,—
Some artful knaves to mischief prone,
Who long had mark'd their clamorous tone,
Assiduous fann'd the rising flame,
And urg'd them on to try their game ;
Nor urg'd in vain,—for, keenly stung,
The taller from the settle sprung,
And at the other aim'd a blow,
With force to lay a bullock low :
But he, too wary, duck'd his head,
The wall receiv'd the blow instead,—
Then, at his staggering foe let fly,
And ting'd his cheeks with crimson dye :—
Soon both fell heavy on the floor,
And kick'd, and thump'd, while tumbling o'er ;
Now others mingled in the fray,
Their pretext—to maintain fair-play ;

And louder still the discord rose
From brawling tongues, and sounding blows,
The landlord's firm, commanding call,
And females' screams, that pierc'd through all;
Confusion reign'd, in wildest mien,
And hasty ruin strew'd the scene,—
Seats, tables, smash'd, fell limb from limb,—
With ale, and blood, the floor did swim,
While madmen fought, with wounds o'erspread,
And bodies sprawling stretch'd, as dead.
Watch! watch! was call'd,—the watchman came
With cudgel stout, their wrath to tame,
And, dealing round a hearty crack,
He brought their wandering senses back,—
When all, who could, ran off in fear,
Regardless who the cost should clear.

In this fierce strife our chosen train,
Of harm had little to complain;
The rake alone had interfer'd,
And he, with blood, was sore besmear'd:
The patriarch, by experience, knew
That woe from discord ever grew,
Withdrawing wisely from the fray,
This Nestor homeward led the way;—

" How vile," cried he, " that men abuse

" What nature meant for wholesome use,

" A joy-inspiring gift of Heaven,

" To comfort weary mortals given ;

" How shameful is all guzzling waste,

" While some can scarce afford to taste,

" Those men, who reason thus resign,

" Deserve the fitting name of swine ;

" And they, who when in drink immers'd,

" Like powder, let their passion burst,

" Or, maim'd, or beaten black and blue,

" Another day their folly rue ;—

" Thus we, without receiving pain,

" From their rash error wisdom gain."

    Though night, in gloom, o'ercast the road,

Their spirits felt no weighty load,

 , In mellow, fear-despising frame,

Returning merrier than they came ;

All, timid bashfulness forsook,

Each youth his favourite damsel took ;

By talk beguil'd, and lively sport,

The long black march appear'd but short :

Fair Susan, and her goodly swain,

Breath'd forth, apart, the fervent strain ;

With joys, which only lovers know,
Again they pledg'd the sacred vow ;
Their cottage windows, gleaming bright,
Peep'd welcome to the wanderers' sight,
As, from the ancient steeple-tower,
The bell proclaim'd the midnight hour.

THE HOME-EXPELLED BRITONS.

I.

'T is sweet to gaze upon the broad expanse
  Of boundless ocean, in his gentlest mood,
To see the sun's exhilarating glance,
  With orient lustre gild the rippling flood.

II.

How chang'd the scene, when tempests, frowning dire,
  Dash the rude billows 'gainst the rocky shore,—
When breakers rave, with unrelenting ire,
  And daunt the tar, who ne'er was mov'd before.

III.

Hard is the task, to nerve the wavering heart
  To brave the perils of the faithless sea ;
When forc'd from this dear island to depart,
  Impell'd by stern necessity's decree.

IV.

View yon fam'd port, on Britain's western coast,
  Teeming with industry and bustling trade,—
What stores and shipping there, a nation's boast,
  What wealth, and state, on every hand display'd.

V.

But, painful contrast! yon sad pilgrims mark,
  Of every class, that throng the busy strand ;
Searching, with eager glance, for some kind bark
  To bear them safely to a foreign land.

VI.

Far, 'mid the spacious regions of the West,
  Won by Columbus—victor o'er the waves,
They hope to find a land with plenty bless'd,
  Since this denies the comforts nature craves.

VII.

Their stores secur'd,—to all they value most
  They sigh adieu !—for time nor tide will stay ;
The signal given,—each tar assumes his post,
  The canvass spreads ;—the vessel cleaves her way.

VIII.

Turning from fortune's frown to court her smile,
  The wanderers, fast receding from the shore,
Cast one fond look on Albion's sea-girt isle,
  That land belov'd, which they may see no more.

IX.

And why are these, like exiles, doom'd to roam
  Beneath strange skies, 'mid rocks and forests wild?
Sever'd from kindred ties, and friends, and home,—
  Sweet hills and vales, where their first morning
    smil'd?

X.

This favour'd land, why leave they? which displays
  Such beauty, grandeur, plenty, wealth, around,—
Whose scenes so lovely strike the' admiring gaze—
  The hills with wood, the vales with verdure crown'd?

XI.

The cause, alas! their looks evince too plain,
  Want pales the cheek—depression sways the soul;
Ills following ills, have burst—a dreadful train—
  And heavier clouds above still darkly roll.

XII.

In vain may bounteous Harvest deck the field,—
  Her sail, in vain, proud Commerce may expand,
If labour's hard-earn'd pittance will not yield
  The humble store man's craving wants demand.

XIII.

If thus the flower of Britain leave her shore, *
  Her skill'd mechanics and her hardy swains,
Whose hands shall yield us every welcome store,
  Or robe with plenty our forsaken plains?

XIV.

In humble life, what mournful scenes prevail!
  Distress expands her sable pinions there;
The springs of virtue—peace—contentment—fail,
  And Hymen's torch burns with a feebler glare.

XV.

But say, can man, when tender passion sways,
  Though cares may daunt, its pleasing force restrain?
On smiling beauty can he fondly gaze,
  And sunder'd from his highest bliss remain?

XVI.

Lo! the warm youth, and maiden blushing fair,
  To whom few joys the nuptial-state can bring,
Who prove no raptures unalloy'd by care,
  How low their hopes in life's gay blooming spring.

XVII.

Are thus thy pleasures fled, inspiring Love?
  Sweet solace destin'd to mankind below;
Who brightly shed, on Eden's flowery grove,
  Warm'd our first parents with thy genial glow?

XVIII.

Thy alter'd form—how humbling to behold!
  From that primeval lustre, sweet and pure;
Too often barter'd now for sordid gold,
  Too oft the prize of splendour's dazzling lure.

XIX.

" In life's low vale," how many fondly sigh,
  Nor dare fulfil the heaven-ordain'd decree;
The sacred nuptial-bond afraid to tie,
  Dismay'd by thoughts of chilling penury.

XX.

Oh Britain! Queen of Ocean!—Europe's pride!—
 The world's dread arbitress,—with glory crown'd,—
Say, must thy sons in hopeless pain abide,
 Can no relief—no healing balm be found?

XXI.

Where now are they? the loudly-vaunting host,
 Who swell'd thy woes, fomenting impious wars?
What now remains for blood and treasure lost,
 But faded glory, burdens, tears, and scars?

XXII.

Was it for this, to stay the couqueror's pace,
 Thy warriors steep'd with gore the Belgic plain?
Was Gaul but vanquish'd that thy plunder'd race
 In deeper penury might drag their chain?

XXIII.

And live there men, by thy rich bounty fed?
 Calling thee mother—ah, unfilial they!
Who see dark ruin thy fair realms o'erspread,
 Nor take one step to check its fearful way?

XXIV.

O ! how can such, proud in their envied sphere,—
  Lavish of wealth, from those they injure, wrung,
Still lend to just complaints no pitying ear,
  Deny their country's woes with erring tongue ?

XXV.

May righteous Heaven the faithful labourers shield,
  Direct their zeal, and crown their noble toil,
Who dare the wrath of frowning storms to yield
  Sweet peace and comfort to their native soil.

XXVI.

Soon, soon, may happier days, auspicious shed
  Their grateful warmth on thee, still cherish'd isle !
So, freed from want, and every cause of dread,
  Thy sons may cheerful toil, thy daughters smile.

XXVII.

All hail, Columbia ! thou, whose rising star
  Shines with glad splendour o'er a western world,
Where, like some friendly beacon, seen afar,
  Young freedom's flag triumphant flies unfurl'd.

XXVIII.

Dear land of refuge! where the brave and free,
   Exil'd from home, a hearty welcome share,
And prove, though hireling tongues have slander'd thee,
   Thy fostering kindness—thy maternal care.

XXIX.

Upborne on fancy's wild and rapid wing,
   I soar across the huge Atlantic's swell,
To lands where noble rivers take their spring,
   Where those whom cities starv'd in plenty dwell;

XXX.

Where towering forests wave their branches high,
   And lakes expand, and mighty cataracts roar,
Secluded haunts, where cheerful labourers ply
   Rude toils, which they might never know before:

XXXI.

There fled ye, my three brethren, from that woe
   Which long o'er Britain held its gloomy reign;
Sternly did ye, like thousands more, forego
   Your much-lov'd isle, a kindlier home to gain.

XXXII.

Ye elder two, life's rising scenes had pass'd
  With ease and comfort, in your own calm sphere;
Thus, are ye, ill-prepar'd to brave the blast
  Of foreign hardships, or of toil severe.

XXXIII.

When commerce flourish'd in your native town,
  By moderate toil ye won a little store;
Fair prospects fled when gloom'd depression's frown,
  And left few hopes that they would flourish more.

XXXIV.

Now, as ye roam, where prompts the unfetter'd will,
  Though Nature's gifts are spread with liberal hand;
Yet oft your hearts recall—home—loving still
  The lost endearments of your native land.

XXXV.

But thou, my brother, youngest of the three,
  Thou, youth of dauntless mien and soaring mind,
Foe to oppression, vigorous, bold, and free,
  Thou scorn'st to cast one homeward look behind:

XXXVI.

Thy warm, impetuous spirit could not bear
  To see such wrongs the sinking land o'erflow,—
Each burden'd drudge denied his well-earn'd share
  Of daily comforts, sunk in want and woe:

XXXVII.

Thy early years were spent in arduous toil,
  (Yet not from learning's humbler stores debarr'd,)
But manual arts, or culture of the soil,
  No comfort left behind—no just reward.

XXXVIII.

Now brighter prospects charm ;—thy bosom's fire
  Glows with fresh ardour through the toilsome day,
In full assurance of a bounteous hire,
  Thy strong, unwearied labours to repay.

XXXIX.

Urging on all, who here their lot deplore,
  To leave a land in chains of misery bound,
Thou bidd'st them welcome to Columbia's shore,
  Where freedom holds her seat, and sheds her bless-
    ings round.   D

GENERAL MEETING AT ACKWORTH SCHOOL.

I.

THIS day, the sweetest of the year,
Hope-lov'd—in memory treasur'd dear—
   Glad-utter'd by each tongue—
When friends, long parted, warmly greet,
And bonds of love, more kindly meet,
   And age once more seems young,—

II.

Tells of a fond-remember'd time,
When life exulted in its prime,
   Here bless'd with golden dreams.
Hail! walls, where peace and joy abide,
Bowers, gardens, cloth'd with Summer's pride,
   And ye mead-loving streams.

III.

Those cupolas,—where morning's smile
Plays bright,—that noble central pile—
   Gigantic in embrace ;
Whose wings on either side extend,
To guard, to cherish, and befriend
   The tender rising race :—

IV.

The green—that sport-inviting ground,
The shed—where skippers lightly bound,
   While whizz their cords in air ;—
To me, like well-known friends, are dear,
Who once was blithe as any here,
   And knew not more of care.

V.

Thought rushes from its secret springs,
While memory swift before me brings
   The scenes of former years ;—
When here the first firm stone was laid,
The virtues lent their holiest aid,
   Mov'd by the foundlings' tears.

VI.

Benevolence, with offer'd dower,
And Pity,—gentle soothing power,
　Smil'd kindly on the place;
And Charity,—of higher birth,
Descending gracious, came on earth
　To feed the helpless race.

VII.

Time saw a change—for here, the mind
As yet in chains of sloth confin'd,
　Assum'd its noble throne:—
A people came—who once withstood
Reproach and hate, while, humbly good,
　They bow'd to One alone:—

VIII.

Here, choosing learning's pleasant seat
Within this order-rul'd retreat,
　They plac'd their offspring dear,—
Who, train'd with care by guardians kind,
Are taught to store with Truth the mind,—
　And her pure laws revere.

IX.

The fair, the serious, the gay,
Plain, neat their garb—are seen to-day—
  Beauty unplum'd is here;
Yet, simpler were their sires of old,
Who, strong in toil, unflinching, bold,
  Walk'd firm, with Truth severe.

X.

Not the bare word, nor barer form,
Sustain'd them in their morn of storm,
  Heaven was their light—their guide;
So long as men on Heaven rely,
They will the worst of foes defy—
  Strife—fraud—ensnaring pride.

XI.

Thus warm my feelings as I gaze
On these dear scenes of early days,
  Where my young mind acquir'd
The seeds of that augmenting store,
Which daily culture ripen'd more,
  While glowing hope inspir'd.

XII.

Yet, here, what hours I mourn as lost:
Since then, by changeful breezes toss'd,
   All lore was laid at rest;
Till late, once more the flame aspir'd,
By some strange secret impulse fir'd,
   Too strong to be repress'd.

XIII.

Where'er around I cast my eyes,
What long forgotten thoughts arise,—
   A rapid, fleeting train:
The well-known grounds I traverse o'er,
Each room—each favourite haunt explore,
   I feel a boy again.

XIV.

The youngsters, eyeing my advance,
With their peculiar schoolboy's glance,
   Their varied sports pursue;
Unknown to me each prying face,
Save that in some a kindred trace
   Of former friends I view.

XV.

All those I knew and valued here,
Still cherish'd in remembrance dear,
  Are gone—their place supplied:
As leaves now bud and now decay,
So these, in turn, enjoy their day,
  And then are scatter'd wide.

XVI.

Thus youth, exulting, starts in life;
While transient joys, and care, and strife,
  And sorrows intervene:
Till Time, with silent, fatal aim,
Assails man's earthly-moulded frame,
  And sweeps him from the scene.

XVII.

But long from you, ye sprightly train,
May gloomy care and wasting pain
  Be kindly far withdrawn:
Your buoyant hopes, your sparkling joy,
I would no storms might e'er destroy,
  Or cloud your smiling dawn.

XVIII.

Soon will the time of trial come ;—
While here you spring in vernal bloom,
   Be every means applied :—
Life's path is rude,—with patient care
The stores your journey claims, prepare
   To comfort and to guide.

XIX.

On you the eyes of friends sincere,—
On you the hopes of kindred dear,
   With deepest interest turn ;
Since they with warmth your welfare seek,
Your thanks let zealous action speak,
   Nor cold such favours spurn.

XX.

First—the young mind, assiduous store,
With rudiments of valued lore ;
   Through learning's portals glide :
When gain'd, her wide and fertile field,
From choicest springs will wisdom yield
   An ever-flowing tide.

XXI.

But, as a long-neglected soil,
Or, as a lamp unfed by oil,
  Or instrument unus'd,—
So, careless minds, more dullness gain,
Acquirements are possess'd in vain,
  And gifts are but abus'd :—

XXII.

As ore, which dross and rust enclose,
The more 't is polish'd, brighter glows ;
  So, by due care, the mind
Expands its powers, acquires new force,
Above the vulgar, gains a source
  Of pleasures, pure, refin'd.

XXIII.

Such minds explore the realms of space,
The secret laws of nature trace,
  And truth and harmony ;
Where earth her loveliest robe displays,
And wondrous scenes awaken praise,—
  The God of Nature see.

XXIV.

Then, let these precious moments flow,
In learning all that man should know—
   Enlarge each active power ;
With truth and virtue store the breast,
On these your firmest hopes will rest,
   In life's declining hour.

XXV.

For, in this fluctuating life,
(Bewildering round of toil and strife,)
   No joys so pure abound,
As those which move in virtue's train :—
'Mid care, and penury, and pain,
   With her content is found.

XXVI.

Truth cheers the righteous on their way,
Calm, while in earthly bonds they stay,
   And bless'd when life is o'er—
Upborne, as on seraphic wings,
The ransom'd soul exulting springs,
   And grief is known no more.

EYMING-WOOD FIELDS.

I.

THE night-shades are vanish'd, and Phœbus, fair
    beaming,
  His light and his-cheerfulness yields;
I haste, while his rays through the thin clouds are
    streaming,
  To summon my charge from the fields.

II.

To fresh-renew'd vigour by sweet rest restored,
  The steeds raise their ears at my call;
The milk-beasts, as though the kind hand they im-
    plored,
  Now lowing advance to the stall.

III.

Before me dark Eyming is gloomily bending—
  So dear to each youth and each maid:

He towers like a rampart, these pastures defending,
   And flings o'er the glebe his broad shade.

IV.

In the full glow of boyhood the sons of diversion
   Oft hie down the skirts of this wood,
To greet their warm limbs with a cooling immer-
   sion,
   And sport in the smooth bracing flood.

V.

The wood-songsters carol their heart-soothing num-
   bers,
   Amid the' embowering trees ;
The dew-drops smile bright, (gently wak'd from
   night's slumbers,)
   Like pearls from the orient seas.

VI.

Around me the harvest is briskly advancing ;
   No longer the clouds swell with rain :
The swains blithe repair, while the warm rays are
   glancing,
   To gather the golden-ear'd grain.

VII.

Health, peace, my attendants, while Summer shone
    brightly,
  I've toil'd 'midst the fragrant new hay;
While youths and gay damsels, with converse so
    sprightly,
  Have banish'd reflection away.

VIII.

But the scene now reminds me, as here I stand gazing,
  Our sweet rural labours are o'er ;—
And from these very fields, where our cattle are
    grazing,
  We share the full harvest no more.*

IX.

Should evil days tear us from yon habitation,
  The haunt of our infancy bless'd ;
Though the young with more firmness might bear
    separation,
  Ah! where could the aged find rest?

---

* This land is now given up.

X.

But cease ! ye fond flowings of tender emotion,
  I'll muse with a resolute mind ;
For should I be driven to cross the wild ocean,
  Yet Hope even then may be kind.

XI.

What led you, my brothers, to take your departure
  For distant Columbia's shore ?
The best bulwark there,—is it Liberty's charter ?
  Proud wrong,—sleeps he yet in his gore ?

XII.

When the land of your fathers no more could be-
    friend you,
  'T was then, this fair land you resign'd ;—
And now, in your toils, though slight hardships
    attend you,—
  ·Sweet peace and abundance you find.

XIII.

O England! should freedom's true day-star, ascending,
  E'er beam on thy green fertile shore,

Thy pale drooping sons, now with misery contending,
  Would think of removal no more.

XIV.

When, selfishness spurning, thy rulers endeavour
  To foster the weal of the state,
And crush all the systems, oppressive, which sever
  The humble in life, from the great;—

XV.

When Truth reigns triumphant, undimm'd in her
    shining,
  When labour with plenty is crown'd,—
Then joy and contentment will banish repining,
  And Peace shed her blessings around.

GREENFIELD HILLS.

I.

Noting each change of scene, of men as well,
  I pace, where rugged tracts around me lie,
Through Saddleworth, bleak land of hill and dell,
  Whose toiling race, the marts of trade supply.
  The stunted shrubs, and o'er me rearing high,
The heath-rob'd hills, blend each Autumnal hue :—
  Afar I hear the loud-resounding cry
Of eager hounds, that chase the fearful hare—
  And now, I see the ardent sportsmen throng
'Mid the wild scenes, undaunted, void of care—
  Borne by the breeze, now swells the echo strong,
  Now, sinking, dies away, the distant hills among.

II.

But lo ! dark-brooding, o'er the horizon dim
  Yon heavy cloud forewarns me to retire ;

The hunter quails not, storms are nought to him,
   They cannot quench his fiercely-glowing fire ;—
Then, let him gratify his soul's desire, .
   A friendly cot I seek, ere every limb
   Feels the chill moisture, through my wet attire :
With the free natives of this region rude
   Till the dark tempest cease will I abide ;
Though lowly born, yet are their breasts endued
   With kindness warm, howe'er their lot supplied—
   Here, native bounty glows, unknown to boastful
     pride.

III.

The rain has ceas'd—I quit this calm retreat,
   And climb the steep whose brow assails the sky ;
Hills, moors, around—deep vales beneath my feet,
   And distant cots, and streams, salute my eye,
   No living creature near me I descry.
Here solitude has fix'd her airy seat ;—
   No sound I hear, save the wild heath-cock's cry,
And the mad torrent dashing down the hill ;
   What rapturous feelings in my bosom roll,—
What glowing thoughts these scenes sublime instil ?
   At this high altar, may the unfettered soul,
   Waft incense pure to Heaven, nor know proud
     man's control.

IV.

Yet vain that search, to find through earth's wide
    bound
  The spot where guilty passions never came ;
I look—creation's grandeur reigns around :—
    On man who stain'd these charms, I think with
    shame.
  Yon cot which lisping babes with terror name,
Where oft the mountain-wanderer comfort found,
    Saw murder—could its stones that guilt proclaim,
There sunk a father, smit by deadly blows,
    Nor could the son himself by valour save—
His wounds were deep, from many cruel foes.
    Hath glory charms ?—let this adorn his grave—
    His was a holy cause—he fell as fall the brave.

V.

The white-wreath'd clouds, that veil'd yon hills afar,
    Mov'd by the rising gust now onwards glide :
Soon, like a host, fierce rushing to the war,
    The winds resistless sweep, a whelming tide.
    Swift fly the vapours ;—now the hills they hide—
And now expose their summits bleak and bare.
    I must descend nor madly here abide,

For mist surrounds me—nought can I survey,
  Save sparkling streams, which rolling, headlong
    leap—
With cautious steps I gain the public way—
  Lest I should sink in moss-grown quagmire deep,
  Or by rude winds be hurl'd o'er some impending
    steep.

IRISH WANDERER.

I.

Since Pity's mild trace is
Display'd on your faces,
Pray hear ! what his case is,
  Who treads on your ground,—
From Ireland just landing,
Whose glory expanding,
Once, bright and commanding—
  Now, faint beams around:
Where nature smiles freely ;
Where praties grow mealy ;
Where verdure springs gaily,
  And sprightly girls smile :
Whose sons with kind dealing,
Are warm-hearted, willing,—
No base heart concealing,
  With hypocrite wile,

Och! the shamrock-crown'd nation,
The pride of creation,
Is valour's high station,
  And honour is law;
Though foes trample o'er us,
All true hearts deplore us,
And join our sweet chorus,
  Our " Erin go bragh."

II.

Behold me first enter,
On life's wild adventure,
My kind parents centre
  In me all their joy:
By them fondly cherish'd,
And plenteously nourish'd,
I grew and I flourish'd,—
  A fine hopeful boy!
My powers ripen'd early,
I priz'd mirth sincerely,
I lov'd the girls dearly,
  And dear they lov'd me.
Ere gain'd my full stature,
I join'd a sweet creature,
In mind and in feature
  From all blemish free.

III.

Our union cemented,
A snug cot we rented,
And there liv'd contented,
  Unconscious of gloom :
Till evil's dark hour,
Did stormily lour ;
When Erin's green bower,
  Was stripp'd of its bloom.
Then toil naught avail'd me,
My wages soon fail'd me,
Hard stewards assail'd me,
  Though famine rag'd wide.
Stern law's harpies teasing,
The titheman so fleecing,
Our scanty stores seizing,
  With insolent pride.

IV.

Thus plunder'd my dwelling,
My blood warm was swelling,
My fierce heart rebelling
  'Gainst laws so unjust :
Impetuously springing.
My shillela swinging,

A wretch, with head ringing,
  I laid in the dust.
But justice, unbending,
Her agent defending,
From kindred ties rending,
  Consign'd me to chains:
My wife, tender-hearted,
In anguish long smarted,
Until by death parted
  From wants and from pains.

V.

When freedom I tasted,
My prospects were blasted,
My native isle wasted,
  By ruin's fell hand:
I left lovely Erin,
And kindred endearing,
And heedless went steering
  For Albion's strand.
Now, careless and cheery,
Now, pensive and dreary,
Starv'd, hungry, and weary,
  I wander along:
Now, hopeless—despairing,
Employment now sharing,

And drowning my care in
  Sweet whiskey or song.
For the shamrock-crown'd nation,
The pride of creation,
Is valour's high station,
  And honour is law:
Though foes trample o'er us,
All true hearts deplore us,
And join our sweet chorus,
  Our " Erin go bragh."

TRIUMPH OF PURE LOVE OVER DIFFICULTY.*

I.

PROPITIOUS the breezes are blowing,
   That waft us from Albion away,
The sea—calm and silently flowing,
   Exults in the sun's joyous ray.

II.

Receding art thou from my view,
   Fair Island, my dear native land,
I breathe thee my last fond adieu,
   As lingering I gaze on thy strand!

---

* This Poem was written on the embarkation of an interesting young female—who, at the earnest request of her lover, had the courage to cross the Atlantic to become the sweetener of his toils and the wife of his bosom. She arrived in safety at the humble abode which his strenuous labours had prepared for her in America. The union of the mutually faithful pair was joyfully accomplished. She is here represented as taking leave of her own land. These sentiments, though not really expressed by her, we may readily conceive were not foreign to one who evinced such pure attachment and undaunted magnanimity.

E

III.

Though tears from my eyes are now falling,
　When no more my lov'd home I may see,
A kind voice of comfort is calling
　" Thy joys shall be dearer with me."

IV.

How sweetly it falls on my ear,
　Recalling delights of the past,
'T is the voice of a youth ever dear,
　Whose faith will not bend with the blast.

V.

When childhood's warm feelings were glowing,
　What moments of gladness we prov'd,
While youth's genial current was flowing,
　In converse delightful we rov'd.

VI.

And now, though by sternest decree,
　We widely asunder are torn,
Can aught in my lover and me,
　E'er quench the pure flame, Heaven-born.

VII.

He calls me his home to prepare,
   And cheer him when labour is done,
On a soil where the humblest may share
   The meed which that labour has won.

VIII.

His hope-breath'd request I obey,—
   The task is stupendous I know,—
Though perils encompass my way,
   To his arms of protection I go.

IX.

Though skies in black horror were scowling
   And seas rolling valley and hill,—
Though wildly the tempests were howling,
   Not all could have shaken my will.

X.

Mine is not affection so fleeting,
   That danger can weaken its force,
As the rill and the mountain-flood meeting,
   It gathers new strength in its course.

XI.

Let some who exult in their splendour,
    Unwarm'd by the pure moving flame,
By stooping to interest render
    Their nuptials a contract of shame ;—

XII.

Let some pursue wealth, rank, and beauty,
    Nor know what affection implies,
With fervour to love is my duty,
    The heart is the treasure I prize.

XIII.

Though mirth and profusion abound,
    'Mid the glare of the light festive hall,—
Though honour and grandeur surround,
    Full soon may satiety pall.

XIV.

Love scorns to reside in the soul
    That bows to base lucre a slave,
Remorse soon embitters the bowl,
    Which a moment of ecstasy gave.

XV.

Not so—when two hearts by a tie
    Of mutual affection are bound,
There—love in the tremulous sigh,
    And deep mantling blush may be found.

XVI.

No change, no stern mandate can sever
    That strong and immaculate bond,
Once kindled, their bosoms will ever
    With warmest devotion respond.

XVII.

And oft the low cot will afford
    More bliss than a palace can give,
When parents and offspring accord,
    In humble contentment to live.

XVIII.

To them, while unruffled by strife,
    Flow blessings from Heaven's rich store,
And e'en the afflictions of life
    Will bind their affection the more.

XIX.

But cease, O my wandering thought,
　Nor roam in wide fancies astray,—
Be now my own happiness sought,
　Though distant and arduous the way.

XX.

For like a young bird that has flown
　From parents and fostering nest,
Self-aided, I journey alone,
　My hopes all in Providence rest.

XXI.

The warbler on light flitting wing,
　Soon wooes a congenial mate,
Thus, I in so simple a thing,
　An emblem behold of my state.

XXII.

And now, I bid England adieu!
　To seek the delight of my soul,
Whose heart to its object is true,
　As the magnet is true to the pole.

XXIII.

Though a Mother my absence will weep,
  Though kindred and friends may deplore,
Yet borne on the wide-rolling deep,
  I gaze on my country nó more!

XXIV.

When the soul-cheering beacon of Love,
  In radiance beams to the eyes,
The stories of ages will prove,
  What-dangers are borne for the prize.

XXV.

And lo! where my beacon is streaming,
  Like a light seen afar in a tower,
A star of fair promise, whose gleaming
  With fortitude arms me and power.

XXVI.

While briskly the fresh breathing gales,
  Are hasting our course o'er the sea,
Dear hope in each bosom prevails,
  That prosperous our passage will be.

XXVII.

This prayer warmly springs from my breast,
  " Safe lead me my Helper and Guard,
" To him whom on earth I love best,
  " Here grant me no higher reward :—

XXVIII.

" O teach us with patience to bear,
  " The evils in life which abound,
" That still in each duty and care,
  " Unblemish'd our union be found :—

XXIX.

" Like yon sun in his course overcast,
  " Yet calmly declines as he rose,
" And shines in mild splendour at last,
  " So cloudless, so bless'd be our close :—

XXX.

" As the skies, when his orb sinks from sight,
  " His cloud-tinging pomp long retain,
" May we leave a reflection as bright,
  " As cheering to all who remain :—

XXXI.

" To this all my cares shall be given,
  " In the soft favouring smile, or the frown,
" I trust to thy mercy, O Heaven!
  " My humble endeavours to crown."

REFLECTIONS.

I.

ONCE more I view the lowly vale,
  Where Dearne glides 'neath the alder trees ;
Once more my native roof I hail,
  Where poplars, towering, court the breeze.

II.

How oft have I forsook this home,
  To tread in pleasure's mazy train ;
But soon, perchance, I may not roam
  From these sweet peaceful bounds again.

III.

Here duty stern I now resume,
  And with the eager, bustling throng,

Beneath bright skies, or tempests' gloom,
   Must urge my vigorous steeds along.

IV.

What ! though in Summer's smiling hours,
   I bask'd in pleasure's genial ray ;*
Now must I guard, ere Winter lowers,
   'Gainst penury's chill and bitter day.

V.

Though heartfelt joys with slight cares blended,
   Are mine where'er I fondly roam,
These rugged toils may be attended
   With peace—the sweetest charm of home.

VI.

I've stood beside the boundless deep,
   While sparkling in the sun's glad ray ;—
Have watch'd fair barks majestic sweep,
   Dashing from rolling waves the spray :—

---

* That Summer I had been a considerable traveller; the Piece was composed on resuming employment after the agreeable relaxation.

VII.

I've gaz'd, where rural beauty glows—
   On regions rude, romantic, grand,—
On scenes, where once proud fabrics rose,
   Now mark'd by ruin's mouldering hand ;—

VIII.

I've been, where Health's restoring waters,
   Yielding relief to thousands, spring ;—
Have sat in halls, where beauty's daughters,
   To rapture wak'd the tuneful string ;—

IX.

I've been, where native kindness shone,
   And real friendship warm'd the soul,—
Where soon each heavy cloud was gone,
   O'er me, in blackness, wont to roll :—

X.

But now, those hours so gaily spent,
   No more I vainly call to mind ;
For still sweet heaven-inspir'd content,
   Can make e'en rigid labour kind.

XI.

As Cincinnatus glory-crown'd,
　　Resign'd the glittering meed of power,
With willing hand to till the ground,
　　His father's dear, yet humble dower ;—

XII.

May such an independence burn,
　　Within my breast with constant flame ;
So may I vain temptations spurn,
　　And joys too often stain'd by shame.

XIII.

Though pleasure lull our cares a while,
　　And soothe the aching nerve of toil,—
Yet fly from sloth's corrupting smile,
　　Lest weeds should mar a healthy soil.

XIV.

No Father's aiding hand is nigh,—
　　No Mother's fond regard I share,—
With faultering step, unaided, I
　　Must tread the thorny maze of care.

XV.

Example bright ! those parents kind,
    In all their arduous trials yield ;
Their highest aim—Heaven's path to find—
    And offspring dear, to guide and shield.

XVI.

Warm Charity, and Truth sincere,
    Their unassuming hearts impress'd ;
When clos'd each holy duty here,
    They peaceful sunk to welcome rest.

XVII.

If honour's voice, so false, so vain,
    Applaud these innate powers of mind ;—
Shall I a meed like their's obtain,
    Or, leave so fair a name behind ?

XVIII.

No ! virtue's charms transcendent shine ;
    Good works can never fail ;
If man the Heavenly gift decline,
    What can his brightest powers avail ?

XIX.

His airy dreams, his vain desires,
  Though crown'd, afford no steadfast joy;
Though he exult while fancy fires,
  His baseless, maddening raptures cloy.

XX.

The despot, in triumphant hour,—
  The prelate, with new livings bless'd,—
The courtier, when rich favours shower,—
  The miser glorying o'er his chest;—

XXI.

The wit, the genius, hail'd by fame,—
  The worldly soul, augmenting gain,—
The victor, for a laurell'd name,
  Proud prancing o'er the crimson'd plain;—

XXII.

Though these to crown their hopes attain
  The joy so eagerly pursued,—
Too soon they know their triumph vain,
  For still oppressive cares intrude.

XXIII.

How happier they, whate'er their state,
   Who, in all time, adhere to right,—
Their words, their actions regulate
   By sacred Truth's revealing light ;—

XXIV.

Who serve that Power which bade them live,
   Assist and love their fellow men,—
Who, in their earthly dealings, give
   The measure they would share again ;—

XXV.

Who ne'er Religion's fair attire
   Assume, an evil heart to hide,—
Who ne'er, from venal hopes, aspire
   The peaceful flock of Christ to guide ;—

XXVI.

Who never, by ambition led,
   By rapine, hate, or sordid gain,—
Destruction, want, and misery spread,
   Nor spurn their brethren with disdain ;—

XXVII.

Who ne'er an envious tongue employ
  To vilify a nobler breast,—
Who ne'er by guile, or crime, destroy
  A spotless name—a parent's rest ;—

XXVIII.

Who, ere another they reproach,
  Cleanse their own breast of deeper sin,—
Who let no grovelling cares encroach,
  Uprooting love and peace within :—

XXIX.

In all the shocks of this vain world,
  Though ruin strike his fellest blow,—
Though thrones and powers are prostrate hurl'd,
  Or nations to oppression bow :—

XXX.

Though rude afflictions round them rise,—
  Though men prove slanderous, base, unkind ;—
Yet then they hold the dearest prize,
  A sure consoling peace of mind.

XXXI.

This holy peace, all joys exceeding,
  Not only gilds their path below,—
But still to brighter worlds is leading,
  Where tears of sorrow never flow :—

XXXII.

Those glorious realms by faith are shown ;
  And trusting Heaven's presiding care,
They humbly hope, when time is flown,
  To live in bliss eternal there.

TRIBUTE OF CONSOLATION.

I.

Sᴇᴇ mildly breaking o'er the eastern sky,
  The golden splendour of the morn is spread :
But mark! the gathering vapours as they fly,
  O'er its bright pomp, a sudden darkness shed :
Lo! from meek violet, to fiery red,
  All hues adorn the rich ethereal bow—
It dying fades, and every trace is fled :—
    So earthly hopes, by fancy painted, glow,
    Till rudely sweeps the storm their fleeting glory
      low.

II.

Though man must like his gilded hopes expire,
  He heedless dances on life's changeful stream ;
Now lighted up, his frame, his soul, on fire,
  Now sunk in gloom, and misery extreme :
And though from Heaven unceasing favours teem,
  Yet black rebellion doth his heart enthral ;

While judgment frowns, he, wrapp'd in maddening
dream,
Beholds like leaves, his brethren 'round him fall;
He shrinks aghast from death—but wakes not at
the call.

III.

There is a humble pile, where late were bless'd,
A worthy pair in fondest union tied,
One glowing love inspir'd each answering breast,
Where neither wish'd that mutual flame to hide:
Three playful children flourish'd at their side,
And charm'd the hour, when arduous labours
cease ;
To nourish these, they toil'd with honest pride,
Happy to see their comforts still increase :
Contentment bless'd the cot, and sweet consoling
peace.

IV.

And I, who love a calm retreat like this,
Before the proud, the gay, yet heartless scene,
Have oft, at evening, shar'd their homely bliss,
While intellectual stores our feast have been :

Whene'er I stepp'd within that mansion clean,
   A pleasing smile would bid me welcome there,
While beam'd attention on each sprightly mien,
   With kindred hearts assembled, I did share
   Rich streams of social joy, too pure to blend with
     care.

V.

There came a change,—a gloomy change, for all—
   The hand of God prevail'd in wrath around;
On the sweet Wife the stroke was doom'd to fall,
   Which swift infix'd a deep and cureless wound.
One day beheld her lively, active, sound,
   But on the next she cold and livid lay,
The third, immur'd her relics in the ground:
   As frowns a hideous dream, and flits away,
   So dreadful came her fate—the cruel shock will
     stay.

VI.

Ye smiling babes, that like fair olives grew,
   No longer now a mother's fondness share;
She in her last sad moments thought of you;
   And with a look, which none unmov'd could bear,

Save they whose breasts with rigid steel compare,
   Exclaim'd with fervour to a mourner near,
" What will you do for these who claim your care?"
   The sacred tie which bound in life so dear,
   In death's dread presence held, through agony
     severe.

VII.

Yet, there is one, your Father, he will heed
   That fond injunction, and will still supply,
So far as mortal can, your every need,
   Nor close cold ears upon your plaintive cry:
And while he strives his moisten'd cheek to dry,
   May haply in your opening features, trace
Her look, whose loss, hath dimm'd his watery eye:
   .This with new strength his trembling nerves will
     brace,
   Life still an object yields—earth yet presents a grace.

VIII.

And thou, dear sufferer ! who beheld'st so soon,
   Thy lovely prospect, wasted of its bloom ;—
Prize the brief span, thy Maker's precious boon,
   Ere thou art call'd to share thy partner's tomb.

These living pledges urge thee to resume
  Thy wonted energy ;—the task of love
Will sweetly soothe the pensive hour of gloom ;
  As shoot their frames, their yielding minds im-
    prove,
  Nor fit for earth alone, O raise their hopes above.

IX.

Though hard to trace the silent hand which moves,
  The secret causes of our joy or woe,
Know thou the Almighty chastens whom he loves,
  And bids new comfort from affliction flow.
What—though thou bend'st beneath a whelming
  blow,
  And mourn'st a treasure earth can scarce repay ;
Still there is hope, to cheer thy days below ;
  He who relieves the helpless when they pray,
  May dawn on thy dark soul, and chase the cloud
  away.

X.

The artless glee thy boyish years display'd,
  Youth's dreams—the bliss of wedlock, thine so
  late,

Would weigh as nothing, were thy peace but made
  With him, the fount of joy, who rules all fate,
And in rude wilds can smiling realms create:
  Accept his love, for thee so freely shed,
Which gilds not only this brief cloudy state,
  Its voice shall whisper, o'er thy dying bed,
    " Rise, joyful from the dust, with glory on thy
      head."

WRECK OF THE ROTHSAY-CASTLE.

WHAT numerous snares before our feet are spread,
As on life's chequer'd path we faultering tread :
Who boasts of pleasure here and knows no woe?
Who lives secure from ruin's fatal blow?
Death, when he comes, assume what form he will,
War, famine, plague, disease, is hideous still ;
But when he bursts on joy's unclouded hour,
And hurls his shafts with desolating power,—
When unforeseen, on pleasure's flowery path,
He sheds the vials of his quenchless wrath,
Then deeper sorrow shades each troubled brow,
And kindlier words from weeping pity flow :
What horror glooms around ! what fears depress !
What loudly-vented grief! what poignant, mute dis-
    tress !

Such gloom e'en now this isle o'ershadows wide,
For those who sank in Menai's angry tide:
What mind can dictate and what hand can write
The painful records of that fatal night !

F

Methinks I view, slow driving o'er the sand,
The shatter'd bark, whose inmates trembling stand,
While the mad-crested waves, upheaving high,
Roll o'er their heads, an awful canopy;
The blast—the louder cries—burst on my ears,
Grief frantic raves, or melts in gushing tears;
Around the deck in wild embrace they cling,
And press more closely as new dangers spring,
While cold despair doth on that accent dwell,
Which forms with mingling sighs the last farewell.

As the hoarse gales more loud more vengeful
    blow,
With mightier force the' insulting billows flow,
Now dismal vales, and now huge mountains grown,
They rushing dreadful tear the bulwarks down;
And while sad shrieks attend their sudden sweep,
Resistless bear some victim to the deep;
The vessel groaning from each furious blow,
Loud crashing rends and plunges all below.
Through the dim curtain of the night behold
These hapless beings in confusion roll'd,
Their powers exhausting to avert the doom,
Which threatens all with one wide yawning tomb.   :
The stern commander, who all prayers withstood,
Yields to the fury of the prouder flood:

The mother there, whose cries with tempests blend,
Upholds her precious babe 'til both descend ; .
Friends, kindred blending, wives their husbands
    clasp,
They sink—emerge—at every object grasp.—
To boards and fragments cling with fainting power,
But weak their refuge in this trying hour ;
For, as the waves rush wild with wrathful boom,
They sweep some mortal to an awful doom :
Some, chill'd with cold, and stupified with pain,
Resign the hold they can no more retain ;
And calmly some, from earthly succour driven,
With dying prayer, commend their souls to Heaven.
A few with desperate struggles gain the land,
And some are rescued by a generous hand,
They live the tragic story to relate,
And for their friends bewail the stroke of fate,
While in their minds, engrav'd with deepest trace,
They bear what time and change can not erase.
I need not here in mournful numbers tell,
What feelings wild in kindred bosoms swell,
The tender sighs, the sympathizing tears,
The rumours strange, the swift contagious fears,
The rending anguish, and the grief profound,
Which press the hearts of thousands to the ground,

Though they from life and every tie`are torn,
Whose loss so many feel and deeply mourn ;
He who from evil good ordain'd to flow,
In wisdom struck this agonizing blow,
To His eternal will resign'd we all must bow.

WAIL OF THE PROFLIGATE.

I.

RELENTLESS drives the furious blast
  Around my houseless head ;
With clouds whose gloom is deepening fast,
  The skies frown darkly dread :

II.

Yet keener than this blast, the pang
  My own sad feelings dart ;
Though dismal clouds above me hang,
  More horror shrouds my heart.

III.

Once was I bless'd by genial skies,
  Gilding my prospects fair ;
Whate'er the earth's rich womb supplies,
  Was freely mine to share.

IV.

But wealth, which from the wise and good,
  Like wholesome streams, will flow—
Abus'd by folly's lavish brood,
  Is ever found a foe.

V.

Soon as the all-receiving mould
  Had clos'd upon my sire,
Impetuous, warm, and uncontroll'd,
  I loos'd each wild desire.

VI.

Soft pleasure spread her silken snare,
  I chose her flowery way ;
Nor deem'd beneath that surface fair,
  What latent evils lay !

VII.

Boon friends I found—the gay, the vile,
  Who hated sober thought :
In me the harlot's faithless wile,
  A ready victim caught.

VIII.

Spurning religion's calm controul,
  To each known duty blind—
I laid in waste those powers of soul,
  For nobler ends design'd.

IX.

Intemperance, nurse of every vice,
  Most led my heart astray ;
Once drawn upon this dangerous ice,
  My course I could not stay.

X.

Inspir'd by Circe's poisonous draught,
  My spirits wildly flew ;
When low they fell, again I quaff'd,
  Their ardour to renew.

XI.

Now sunk in thoughtless ease, supine,—
  Now whirl'd in folly's stream,
I thought the earth's best joy was mine—
  'T was but a passing dream,

XII.

Which sooth'd me, while the maddening spell
   On each lull'd sense, was shed :
The charm was broke—the rapture fell—
   I woke to grief and dread.

XIII.

Thou God ! who saw'st a creature vile,
   Long tread the rebel's path,
Wert pleas'd thine ill-requited smile,
   To hide a while, in wrath.

XIV.

Illusive riches fled afar
   From one who scorn'd a guide,
And fiercely, ruin's whelming car,
   Roll'd o'er my fallen pride.

XV.

The aid of friends I hop'd to prove—
   No friend, alas ! came near ;
The voice that once breath'd sounds of love,
   Now harshly smote mine ear.

XVI.

The virtuous I had shunn'd before,
　　To them I could not fly,—
The vile, who once had shar'd my store,
　　Now pass'd disdainful by.

XVII.

Compell'd to quit that peaceful home,
　　Which long my sires possess'd,
Far from those dearest haunts to roam,
　　Where childhood's hours were bless'd—

XVIII.

An out-cast on the world's wild scene,
　　I took my dreary way,
With frenzied soul, with sullen mien,
　　Which shunn'd the glance of day.

XIX.

Thus do I wander, stung by shame,
　　And sin-created woes;
While life's once warm and buoyant flame,
　　Now dimly, feebly glows.

XX.

The sensual joys, so rashly sought,
    Left dreadful pains behind ;
Too dearly were those pleasures bought,
    Wild fires which shone to blind.

XXI.

As now, my woe-dimm'd eyes I roll
    On thee, unhallow'd joy!
I start, to think a hag so fonl,
    Should lure me—and destroy.

XXII.

The gilded mask which then conceal'd
    Thy blackness from my view,
Is torn—thy face is now reveal'd,
    In its own hideous hue.

XXIII.

Yet, ah! so long thy guilty ways
    Did I unthinking pace,
That e'en, while horrified, I gaze,
    Still could I thee embrace.

XXIV.

In vain—all hopeful dreams are fled,
 At dire misfortune's blow,
While fiends, tormenting, rise instead,
 Mocking my deepest woe.

XXV.

These rags, the last sad wreck of pride,
 Ill brave the bitter shower;
Cold creeps within the vital tide,
 While raging pains devour.

XXVI.

O'er my torn frame appalling raves
 The tempest loud and drear;
A fragile bark on wintry waves—
 I see no haven near.

XXVII.

On future worlds, while rudely driven
 O'er this, which frowns so wild,
I dread to think—in mercy, Heaven!
 Save! save! thine erring child.

POLAND'S LAST STRUGGLE.

THAT fiery spirit, nurs'd on Gallia's shore,
While flow'd her proudest streets with native gore,—
That curb'd and crush'd a guilty despot band,
Who vainly strove, to rule with iron hand,—
And in low Belgium's slaughter-reeking ground
Spread carnage, fire, and ruin swift around;
Whose voice could each proud German Lord appal,
While Alpine mountains echoed back the call ;—
Which for a moment rous'd the sons of Spain,
And e'en inspir'd Ausonia's abject train ;—
Filling Earth's tyrants with wild rage and dread,
Lest wrath so kindled might contagious spread,
And whelm the systems, which insulting stood,
On prostrate nations—stain'd with patriot blood :—
That spirit still prevails, and yet will reign,
Till Right, triumphant, burst each galling chain.
Now by those streams which lave thy fertile land,
Realm ! once redeem'd by Sobieski's hand,
Where Kosciusko toil'd in vain to stay,
Suwarrow, fiendlike, trampling on his prey ;

What time unthron'd, expos'd to lofty scorn,
(Thy monarch wept—his bleeding Poland torn
To swell the empire of three grasping powers,)
There freedom fires, again wild discord lours.
From Warsaw's walls, and from a nation's ire,
To their cold realms the Muscovites retire ;
The northern tyrant, who would Heaven defy,
Arms his fierce hordes, and slaughter is the cry :
The Poles resolv'd—unyielding as a rock—
On death or freedom—sternly wait the shock.

Secure of conquest, proud the invaders rush
With giant strength, an infant's power to crush ;
As the rough waves dash thundering on the shore,
The Russians charge, while murderous engines roar:
And as the rocky shore " resists the waves,"
So Poland meets them and their fury braves ;
In dread suspense the listening nations wait,
Though many pity, none relieve her state ;
She leads her sons devoted to the war,
And on her breast, is beaming glory's star :
Her deeds will long to future ages tell,
How patriot arms did ruthless power repel ;
In her revives a second Spartan fame,
As baffled Russia shares the Persian's shame.

While in each host, disease holds deadly sway,
I leave them struggling in the horrid fray ;
Yet still dark clouds o'er Poland's cause impend,
And she, though victor, must to numbers bend :
The self-styl'd holy potentates may smile
To see her fall—brief be their triumph vile !
Though fairest realms may wither at their tread,
Yet vengeance sure will reach the guilty head.
They boast the emblems of the Prince of Peace—
His Word bids war and fierce oppression cease :
Loud impious praise their tongues ascribe to God—
While He—o'er murder shakes his fearful rod :
Though earthly wrong, defy weak mortal might,
His judgment stands, who will uphold the right :
He marks what grieves his lowest children here,
To them speaks comfort, to their tyrants fear ;
For all shall learn,—vengeance is his alone,
And guilt shall tremble when his wrath is known.

TRUE FRIENDSHIP.

I.

Thᴇ charms of sweet Friendship, what tongue can
 unfold,
  And all its endearments declare?
'T is a treasure which may not be liken'd to gold—
Though gain'd for a moment—uncertain to hold,
  And, deem'd the more precious, as rare.

II.

A blessing, by wisdom celestial design'd,
  Could we our own Happiness know!
So, o'er this fair world, all harmonious combin'd,
Might brother with brother be social and kind,
  And mutual assistance bestow.

III.

But 't is not that friendship, so smooth and so fair,—
  Assum'd when the motive is gain ;—

Nor the mask, which the vile and the treacherous wear,
To lay for the artless a guilt-woven snare,—
 Unseen, till they writhe from the pain :—

IV.

Nor a thing which is worn, or cast off, like our dress,
 With fortune's wild changeable gale,—
'T is the sacred esteem which true bosoms possess,
That in periods of trial, of joy, or distress,
 With the same glowing force will prevail.

V.

More fair than a glance of the sun's cheering ray,
 When from gloom he emerges to light,
Is the smile in the face of a friend we survey ;
And when it is seen in adversity's day,
 That smile is transcendently bright.

VI.

How lovely is Friendship like this ! how divine !
 Her beauties perpetual bloom—
At morning, at noon, her full brilliance will shine,
She sheds a mild grace on life's gentle decline,
 And solemnly rests on the tomb.

ODE TO HUMANITY.

I.

Sweet Power! celestial in thy birth,
O shed upon this tortur'd earth
  Thy precious soothing balm ;—
Come—cheer us with thy look benign,
More fair than gem from Indian mine ;
In fiercest storm one word of thine
  Will breathe a grateful calm.

II.

While millions groan in anguish deep,
Or loud lament, or silent weep,
  In want's pale thraldom held—
While Commerce droops with harrowing care,
While plague rides baleful on the air,
Leaving swift death, and chill despair,
  By hand Divine impell'd :—

III.

O ! let thy genial spirit rest
On all, with wealth and influence bless'd,
   Teach rigid souls to feel—
For those who sink in misery's tide ;—
Nor selfish joys alone provide,
But use the means by Heaven supplied,
   To spread unbounded weal.

IV.

Where war with gory flag unfurl'd,
Hath desolating ruin hurl'd,
   While nations mourn the blow,—
Let tyrants learn thy Holy Law,
Bid discord cease the world to awe,
Nor dare the impious steel to draw—
   So healing peace may flow.

V.

With Truth's appointed teachers dwell,
Urge them to walk with duty well—
   A Heavenly prize to gain,—
To comfort, not oppress the flock,
Nor seize with hearts like flinty rock,

What labour claims, to brave the shock
  Of want's assailing train.

VI.

In every Christian bosom glow,
Let all who to a Saviour bow,
    Walk humbly with their guide ;
Since Worship's outward, formal plan,
Will not alone suffice for Man,
But like the good Samaritan,
    By love must zeal be tried.

VII.

So Mortals, soften'd by thy sway,
May blissful live their fleeting day,
    And mutual suffering heal ;—
The Widow may no more complain,
Nor Orphan raise the piteous strain,
Nor sickness press the bed of pain,
    Without a heart to feel.

VIII.

With thee, the drooping mourner's friend,
May true Religion's light extend,

And clouds of error clear ;
That so, on earth, the Just may prove
A foretaste sweet of Joys above,—
The cruel foe may melt in love,
   The scoffer, learn to fear.

THE HAPPY SURPRISE.

I.

WHERE flowers in eve's calmness repos'd,
  On a bank by green hawthorns o'erhung,
Sat a maid, as the day mildly clos'd,
  Who sweetly yet mournfully sung :—

II.

How long has my William delay'd,
  His joys to blend dearly with mine;
When his vows with such fervour were made,
  Why still the lov'd union decline?

III.

When fatigued by the toils of the day,
  With me this lone walk he pursued,
How oft would he rapturously say,
  That I his worn spirits renew'd.

IV.

Is the flame that was glowing so bright
   Extinguish'd to waken no more?
Or, am I less fair in his sight,
   Or, my heart less warm than before?

V.

No: still his affection for me
   Is constant, devoted, and warm—
Whatever their qualities be,
   None other his bosom can charm.

VI.

But the shadows of love-blighting care,
   Float sad o'er his prospects of joy,—
Hence delays my light spirits impair,
   And hope's soothing visions destroy.

VII.

Though the floweret bloom gaily a while—
   Its hues the fierce tempest may blight;
Though the sun doth now joyously smile—
   His glory must yield to the night.

VIII.

So, beauty should charm ere 't is fled,
  Nor give out its sweetness in vain,—
And love its felicity shed,
  While brightness and fervour remain.

IX.

Soon the bloom on my cheek will decay,
  The warmth in my bosom expire—
If anguish and chilling delay,
  Should freeze the young springs of desire.

X.

" Ah ! no love—thy wailing forbear,"
  —Cried a youth who now stood by her side;
" Dost thou think that soft bosom to tear,
  " One thought in this heart could abide ?

XI.

" For thou art the sole earthly prize,
  " Which, toiling, I sigh to obtain ;
" The flame which affection supplies,
  " Unwasted shall cheer thee again."

XII.

We met, we convers'd, and we lov'd,
  —Resolv'd nought our union should stay,
Still Prudence my ardour reprov'd,
  And, bade me consider the way.

XIII.

I ponder'd, then strove with new zeal—
  Though as yet only small is my store,
If the pain which I gave, I can heal,
  Now take me, I'm thine evermore.

XIV.

True love, all-subduing, will slight
  The dull calculations of care;
Lo! joy's hopeful shore, in our sight—
  Heaven grant that our voyage be fair!

A GLANCE AT STUDLEY AND HACKFALL.

I.

How happy he whose pressing cares
  A short but kind vacation yield ;
Who quits his wealth-returning wares,
  To stray in Nature's boundless field :
Where griping avarice hath not steel'd,
  Nor sinful pleasure stain'd the heart,
Her noblest works, to all reveal'd,
  A sweet unfailing joy impart.

II.

Let minds which nought but wealth can move,
  These uncorrupted joys deride—

G

When leisure grants, be mine, to prove
  Their pure and unexhausted tide :
Ye free, congenial souls, denied
  By duty's call, my walk to share ;
Let me in fancy be your guide
  Through regions wondrous, wild, or fair.

III.

From ancient Ripon's peaceful walls,
  By whispering hope, behold me led,
Where Lawrence views from Studley's halls,
  Around, her blooming Eden spread.
I pass the friendly gate, and tread
  Along the noble avenue,
Where stately trees wave o'er my head,
  Rejoicing in their Summer's hue.

IV.

To trace the art-embellish'd scene,
  I traverse with the ready guide
Fair walks, 'mid bowers of evergreen,
  And grounds with floral charms supplied—
Smooth lawns, where lucid waters glide,
  Here broad expand—there dashing flow ;

And polish'd forms in sculptur'd pride,
  Are imag'd in the wave below.

V.

And all throughout th' enchanting ground
  Are vistas opening to the light ;
Towers, streams, and uplands verdure-crown'd
  Burst forth, and now elude the sight ;
While art's fair-moulded forms invite—
  Life and its varied passions show,
Breathing fell rage, or soft delight,
  Or, drooping in expiring woe.

VI.

What raptures in the soul prevail,
  When bursting from the sweet " surprize,"*
Lo ! in the wood-embower'd dale,
  The old majestic Abbey rise.
The feeble muse but vainly tries
  To image this transporting scene,
Where solemn grandeur strikes the eyes,
  And beauty smiles in richest mien.

---

* The folding-doors through which Fountain's Abbey is seen.

VII.

This ground awakes a holy fear,
  Which sainted men of yore have trod;
Who, bowing low, to rules severe,
  Vow'd to renounce their all, for God—
Beneath the cold, grass-waving clod,
  Their bones are mingled with the clay,
And rapine at a despot's nod,
  Hath laid their walls in sad decay.

VIII.

Soft luxury, in rosy bloom,
  Long ere they fell, corrupting came:
And sin, which hastes a nation's doom,
  Branded a hallow'd class with shame.
But this a lesson may proclaim
  To us, who will not judgment fear;
Nor serve that Power with purest flame
  Whose hand to help is ever near.

IX.

This pile, while art can yield delight,
  Will man revere with homage due:

Proof of his noble skill and might—
  His empty fleeting glory too.
Ye fair, ye solemn haunts adieu!
  So deeply on my mind impress'd,
On you, whatever scene I view,
  Will memory turn and fondly rest.

X.

I leave this fairest spot behind,
  Where art hath lent her choicest aid;
And now through ruder grounds I wind, ,
  Which thickening woods romantic shade:
As in Columbian realms display'd,
  Such darkening verdure here doth wave;—
Mingled with crags, in horror laid,
  O'er dingles deep, where waters lave.

XI.

Hackfall, within thy wondrous bound,
  Rude Nature's throne! I musing tread;
I pace thy winding paths around,
  With darkly-woven boughs o'erspread: ˙
Where streams from o'er their stony bed,
  Or here, in gentler currents creep;

There waterfalls, by gladness led,
   Steal brightly down the mossy steep.

XII.

With arduous step the hill I climb,
   And resting by those rugged walls,
Which frown like towers of elder time,
   The eye on scenes of grandeur falls;
While joy in sounds unnumber'd calls,
   The mountain pathway I descend;—
Beneath, the gushing streamlet brawls,—
   Above me, fearful crags impend.

XIII.

In the lone glen, embosom'd deep,
   Neat domes and cooling grottos lie,
Against the rocks, with furious sweep,
   The rapid Ure is rolling by:
Again the upward course I try;—
   This last exploring effort made,
From Mowbray's point exalted high.
   Too well are all my toils repaid.

XIV.

How can their joy be truly told,
   Who earn before they share the prize?—
Such joy is mine, as I behold
   The prospect which around me lies:
Woods, ting'd with Summer's deepest dyes,
   Hang darkly o'er the sloping height,
Huge frowning rocks tremendous rise,
   Exulting in unshaken might.

XV.

Low in the wild sequester'd dell,
   The Ure's glad waters sparkling play,
While dashing falls the concert swell,
   And songsters chaunting on the spray:
I turn, and wider tracts survey,—
   Towers, cots, and smiling cultur'd ground;
Till scenes in distance fade away,
   Where blue-ridg'd hills the landscape bound.

XVI.

Delightful haunts! the thought how dear,
   With you in studious peace to dwell,

Far from the crowded maddening sphere,
  Where passions rage and discord fell ;
E'en now my heart in holy spell
  Subjected bows to Nature's King ;
Whose voice did Heaven's fair orbs propel,
  And bade this earth in beauty spring.

FAREWELL TO PINDER OAKS.*

I.

How green the budding trees that grow
    Round this sequester'd pile;
And, cheer'd by Phœbus' kindest glow,
    How fair the prospects smile:

II.

But I must quit these shady bowers,
    Where songsters warble sweet,—
These cultur'd grounds, where opening flowers
    Are springing 'neath my feet;

---

* Written before the departure of the family of L. T. Crossley, to Liver-
pool; and supposed to be spoken by the nurse-maid to the children.

III.

And ye fair tender plants that grew
And bloom'd congenial here,
How will the parting prove to you
From scenes to childhood dear ?

IV.

Sweet flaxen-headed cherubs, give
To these your last farewell ;
Nor at the final moment grieve
With sorrow's plaintive swell.

V.

For soon, full soon, we must forsake
These fields and gardens gay ;
From native haunts a journey take
To regions far away :

VI.

Where trade's stupendous fabrics rear
Which tell our country's might ;
Where dashing surges lull the ear,
And grandeur charms the sight ;—

VII.

And there, where commerce spreads her store
   And splendid mansions shine,
Where wealth-crown'd waters lave the shore
   Must be your home and mine.

VIII.

Yet oft 'mid fashion's dazzling glare
   In lone or public walks,
The kindling fancy, borne on air,
   May rest with " Pinder Oaks."

IX.

Adieu, ye fields,—ye smiling bowers,—
   Thou, lov'd abode, adieu!
And oft shall we recall the hours,
   So gaily passed in you.

WELCOME TO A GOLDEN GIFT.*

I.

Thou bonny, shining piece of gold,
Thy form, how pleasing to behold!
But dearer in my hand to hold,
    And doubly pleasant
When I by bounteous tongue am told
    Thou art a present.

II.

Illuming these dark times of woe,
Thy presence bids my bosom glow;
A generous friend did thee bestow
    For rhyming lays

---

* I had intended to have rejected this momentary play of fancy;—the
subject being so sordid, the author may be accused of sordid motives in
publishing it. I am, however, persuaded to risk censure; and I am very
willing that the uncontaminated alone shall condemn me.

Pour'd from my brain with artless flow,
Which won his praise.

III.

And more substantial, dearer still,
With thee too well he crown'd my skill,
Though praise can rapturous joy instil,
    Yet coin so bright,
Deny, I neither can nor will,
    Yields more delight.

IV.

From El-dorado issuing forth,
Or Mexico's rich yielding earth,
Or in what region was thy birth?
    Thou tell'st me not:
But such a piece of sterling worth
    Ne'er bless'd my lot.

V.

Though narrow, envious minds decry,
That humble calling Poesy,—
Yet, when comparison I try,
    With labour hard,—

Long might I drudge and sweat and sigh,
    For less reward.

VI.

Thou great and unexpected fee,
Thus proving doubly dear to me,
No spendthrift now possesses thee—
    Due bounds exceeding:
A hopeful nest-egg shalt thou be,
    While more are breeding.

VII.

'T is not that I incline to hoard—
Nor that I need for bed and board;
That earth for me may such afford
    In future store,
Is all for which I e'er implor'd,
    Or will implore.

VIII.

Ere this rich comfort kindly shone,
Each bard-lov'd smile of favour gone,

I wak'd my rude harp's trembling tone,
    But for my pleasure:
Now more I feel, nor blush to own
    The love of treasure.

IX.

This love predominates in all
Who rule, or serve,—who speak, or scrawl;
And wealth-ennobled beings call
    The world their own:
They soar aloft while others fall
    Unmourn'd, unknown.

X.

Thou art the tradesman's fondest dream,—
For thee the stores of commerce teem,—
For thee is practis'd every scheme,
    With zeal and spirit:—
For thee flows many a studied theme
    Of various merit.

XI.

What thoughts dost thou command to spring—
Thou hope of all—life's leading string;

That with the peasant, peer, or king,
    Still reign'st supreme :—
My soul might soar, on endless wing,
    O'er such a theme.

XII.

Then welcome to my little store,
Thou precious all-commanding ore;
For thee I'll twang with tenfold power,
    The wild harp's string;
For praise, when I can gain no more,
    Content I'll sing.

XIII.

While bless'd with thee I will defy
The howling blast of penury;
And when my breast shall heave a sigh
    Of secret grief,
Thy glories, glancing on my eye,
    May yield relief.

TO AN EARLY FRIEND

ON A LONG SEPARATION.

I.

TORN from thy friend—my loss severe—
What can repair? who now will cheer?
And yet no fond relieving tear
  Is from its fountain starting.
As though impatient to divide
The bond which early friendship tied,
How swift the eager moments glide,
  At this our final parting.

II.

But not in hopeless gloom we mourn ;—
However high, or humbly born,
All, all, must feel some grievous thorn—
  While on this rude earth pacing :
Though in our transitory sphere,
A while dark tempests rage severe,
Kind gleams at intervals appear,—
  Far hence the blackness chasing.

III.

So far as memory can retrace,
When childhood dawn'd in morning's grace,—
When hope display'd a cloudless face,
  Our hearts, our joys were blended.
One home, our various wants supplied,
We bloom'd like plants in vernal pride;
The same kind care our steps to guide—
  We life's wild steep ascended.

IV.

While lightly wing'd the infant hours,
Joy wanton'd in our native bowers;
We twin'd the simple wreath of flowers—
  Rich fruits their sweets bestowing:
When fir'd by boyhood's wilder blood,
We rang'd the mead and tangled wood,
And plung'd amid the cooling flood,
  While Summer suns were glowing.

V.

We trod together learning's field,
And shar'd the joys her fountains yield,

While knowledge to our minds reveal'd
　A glimpse of richest treasures.
From thence to labour snatch'd away,
We, doom'd in ruder walks to stray,
But faintly prov'd fair learning's ray,
　And youth's fond-imag'd pleasures.

VI.

Too much to dreaming folly prone,
The world's strange arts to me unknown,
No cheering beam around me shone
　To light a path so dreary.
But thou, more skill'd, wert cheer'd a while
By hopes which shed a fleeting smile:—
Those hopes are dark—now from our isle
　Thou roam'st a pilgrim weary.

VII.

Between thee and thy native shore,
When forests wave, and wild streams roar,
And ocean lifts his breakers hoar,
　Oft on thy bosom stealing,—
The scenes which charm'd in life's sweet morn,
Though far from their attractions torn,

Will then, by active memory borne,
    Awake a tender feeling:—

VIII.

The bounds wherein thy childhood play'd,
The fields and groves thy light feet stray'd,
The haunts of lore, and bustling trade,
    The friends who much deplore thee,—
Who o'er thee oft delighted hung,
While innate wit flow'd from thy tongue,
These thoughts in vivid colours sprung,—
    Will rapidly come o'er thee:

IX.

Here let me cease this weak lament,
Resign'd to bear what Heaven hath sent;
The last, last moment now is spent,
    Which our close tie must sever.
Across yon ocean's roaring swell,
With thee may high protection dwell;
In all thy wanderings fare thee well,
    My heart shall prize thee ever.

TRIBUTE TO THE GENIUS OF BURNS.

I.

Poor Burns! though oft the 'plaint of gloom,
Hath mourn'd thy hapless, early doom,
I place on thy dear honour'd tomb,
    My offering slight;
Where flowers through time shall sweetly bloom,
    And know no blight.

II.

Who charms like thee, in modern day,
Of all that try the varied lay?
Like thee, who shakes the bigot's sway,
    The proud one's might?—
Or, wounds with satire's fearful play,
    The foes of Right?

ON THE LOSS OF A PROMISING
YOUTH.

WHEN some dear youth, adorn'd with outward grace,
And rich with noblest treasures of the mind,
Smit by the touch of lingering disease,
Which treacherous glides and scarcely seems to
    smite;—
His form, still shrinking with a gradual waste,—
His cheeks, where health late blooming sat,
Now thin, and pale, sad token of decay:—
When he, by hope's last gleam deserted, sinks
Beneath the stroke of all-triumphant Death,
How cruel to the parents is that hour!
With nurture kind, they rear'd his goodly frame,
And planted in his tender mind, the seed
Of fruitful knowledge; and they watched with care,
And saw with joy, a parent's fondest joy,
Fair buds, expanding on the precious youth,
Bright with the promise of a glorious harvest.

How mourn those hearts which friendship's pleas-
    ing bond,
Had knit with his ; who in the flowery vale
Of infancy had play'd, and in the pride
Of glowing youth had shar'd their joys, with him.

To friends and kindred weeping o'er his dust,
What gentle voice shall whisper soothing peace?
A few brief years he shone—their star of hope ;
Then gather'd dark the clouds, the tempests rag'd ;
And he who might have lustre shed on earth,
Is shrouded low in deep involving gloom.
Yet haply then may resignation say :—
" That power which wakes the still, cold clay to life,
Hath hence in wisdom call'd this much-lov'd youth,
To change a stormy for a genial sky,—
The vale of suffering, for the mount of bliss."

H

TO M——

————————————

I.

WHY dost thou ask, engaging fair!
   To hear my lowly strain;
When Winter, desolate and bare,
   Extends his icy chain?

II.

Now when the warbling summer-throng,
   To warmer climes have flown;
And none, save Robin, pours his song,
   All cheerless and alone.

III.

Like him, beneath th' inclement sky,
   I wake a feeble lay;
Thy sweet commands, who would deny?
   I dare not disobey!

IV.

For, as the sun through gloomy skies,
　　Darts forth one moment bright ;
So, shed those lively-glancing eyes
　　O'er this dull season—light ;

V.

Fair Hope, which in the darkest scene
　　Relieves our painful toil ;
And plants her hardy evergreen
　　On Winter's dreary soil ;—

VI.

Now beams auspicious on my soul,
　　And forward bears my view—
Ere many moons will circling roll,—
　　To storms and gloom adieu !

VII.

Blithe Spring will then, in virgin bloom,
　　Deck upland, grove, and vale ;
Sweet flowers will blush, and give perfume
　　To morn's enlivening gale.

VIII.

From budding copse and stately tree,
  Will nature's music rise;
The notes of love ascending free,
  Whilst joy around replies.

IX.

The lovers of the wood and field
  Will, fondly musing, stray;
While genial suns their glories yield,
  To make creation gay.

X.

Dear maid, as thus through change we tread
  Our pilgrimage of pain,
Will Hope, her genial comfort shed—
  Our trembling powers sustain.

XI.

Be this our aim, to walk aright,
  As she our path illumes;—
Revealing climes for ever bright,
  Where Spring unfading blooms.

DAVID'S LAMENTATION.

BEAUTY of Israel! on thy lofty steep,
Thine own hill, slain:—how still the mighty sleep!
Tell not in Gath this foul enduring shame,
Nor in proud Askelon our loss proclaim;
Lest gladness fill the daughters of the foe—
Lest heathen damsels triumph in our woe.
No more Gilboa, on thy gloomy head,
May kindly dews their fostering bounty shed;
No streams of gladness thy cold bosom share,
Nor may first-fruits for offerings flourish there.
For shields of heroes there did vilely fall
The shield of mighty heaven-anointed Saul.
When turn'd the bow of Jonathan from blood?
The sword of Saul, what mortal force withstood?
How pleasant were they in this life,—how fair;
Nor could stern death divide the royal pair:
Their speed out-stripp'd the soaring eagle's flight,—
Their strength surpass'd the lordly lion's might.
Weep, maids of Israel! o'er your monarch's grave,
Ye shine in scarlet, which his bounty gave.

How are the mighty fallen in the fight !
Thou, noble prince, wert pierc'd on thine own height .
Thy loss, my brother, wakes my tenderest grief—
In all my cares, thy kindness gave relief;
What wondrous love thy soul to me inclin'd,—
Love which surpass'd the love of woman kind.
How fell the mighty on the mountain's breast,—
Perish'd the warrior's arms, and bow'd his stately
    crest !

REPROOF OF A WORLDLY SPIRIT.

ECCLESIASTES V.

WALK thou with wisdom to the place of prayer,
Give patient ear, not fools' vain homage there ;
Who think no evil rests upon their head,
And this bare service place in goodness' stead.
Let not rash words from lips unhallow'd fall,
Nor in rude haste upon thy Maker call :
He dwells in Heaven, which mortal cannot see,—
Thou, but on earth, so few thy words must be :
From many cares will rise the troublous dream,
And fools are known where words abundant teem.
To pay thy vows to God be thou not slow,
Who can no joy in thoughtless mortals know :
Redeem thy pledge, nor let a promise sleep—
Better vow not, than vowing, fail to keep.
Let not thy mouth thy flesh to error lead,
Nor to the angel thus for error plead :—
" Why should thy voice offend the mighty God !
O'er thy weak works, why shakes his threatening
    rod ?"

Thy many words, thy many dreams are vain,
But fear thou God, and God will thee sustain.

   Whene'er thine eyes behold the friendless poor,
And all the cruel ills which they endure;
How the land groans, which power, not justice sways,
O let not this thy simple wonder raise!
Though proud ones taunt while injur'd worth com-
   plains,
Yet One regards, who o'er the highest reigns.

   Doth not the earth for all her profit yield?
The king himself is nourish'd by the field.
He that loves wealth, no lasting pleasure proves,
Nor he from plenty, who abundance loves:
When stores increase more to partake them rise,—
What good is wealth unus'd? save to the eyes.
Sweet peaceful sleep, the sons of labour share,
Whether they much partake, or hardly fare:
Are thus the slumbers of the great man bless'd?
No! his abundance tears away his rest.

   Beneath the sun no greater curse is found,
Than riches kept their owner's peace to wound;
These, these, must perish, which his soul adores,—
The son may want, who longs to seize his stores.
Naked as first he caught the beam of day,
Shall he return,—nought can he bear away:

This dreaded lot, the child of earth will find,
Who sighs to grasp, and toiling, grasps—the wind:
He eats his bread, while darkness veils his eyes,
The prey of wrath and sorrow, till he dies.

In all I see, of good and pleasant here,
Sweet is this sight, beyond all others dear ;—
Man, who enjoys what none should him deny,
The good which Heaven and his own hands supply:
And man, endow'd with riches and with power,
Who shares with gladness, the free bounteous shower:
No painful thought recalls his dear-flown days,
Warm thanks his full heart yields, and Heaven re-
    wards his praise.

HONEY WELL.

How dear is the spot where the pure waters flow,
Lov'd haunt,—which the youthful so feelingly know;
O sweet is the sound of the evening breeze,
That murmuring plays through the dark waving trees;
And sweet are the notes of the blithe linnet's song,
That warbles with gladness the green leaves among:—
But sweeter by far is the voice of the maid,
Who lives in yon cottage beneath the cool shade;
With the flowers of that garden no flowers may com-
 pare,
But she who smiles on them is loveliest there.
Since bliss so exalted, I never may know,—
With her, to share all which this earth can bestow,
O may the dear maid in her chosen one find
A mind that is noble, a heart that is kind;
That the smile, playing bright, on their gay bridal
 morn,
May shine, their mild evening of life to adorn.

How guilty the wretch that unfaithful could be,
And coldly a tear on that countenance see.

In friendship alone can I welcome the maid,
When bless'd by her smile I am amply repaid:
Enraptur'd I rove while the sprightly birds sing,
In the meadows and groves near the pure Honey-
Spring.

MORNING CONTEMPLATIONS.

I.

Pure and refreshing flows the breath of morn,—
So kind, it scarcely stirs the flowers of Spring;
The grass-blades shoot—peeps forth the tender corn,
And budding groves with merry anthems ring.

II.

The sweet lark carols, rising from the clod,—
When lost to sight, yet still his numbers charm;
As thus he pours his earliest hymn to God,
My flowing thoughts with kindred rapture warm:

III.

If joy, to hear an unseen minstrel, springs
In worldly souls, what will the righteous feel
When rais'd on meditation's soaring wings,
On their rapt fancy, harps seraphic steal?

IV.

Call it not weak delusion,—when they prove
    Visions of transport on this mournful vale;
Nor my thoughts vain,—which seek to mount above,
    While strains aërial float on morning's gale.

V.

Such joy, before aught earthly, let me share,
    Though fools deride and baneful sceptics sneer;
That time must come, when Truth, supremely fair,
    Will stand triumphant, and her foes shall fear:

VI.

As sure will she dispel each heavy shade,
    That error cast before her holy mien;
As now the sun, in glorious beams array'd,
    Refulgent bursts yon parted clouds between.

VII.

From gazing fondly on the spacious sky,
    Where gold-tints, fading, blend with deepening blue:
Ecstatic rolling, let the fervid eye,
    Below, the works of power Almighty view.

VIII.

Cheer'd by warm rays and friendly showers, the meads
　In robes of fresher, livelier hue are seen ;
Fair smile the woods, as Spring her verdure leads,—
　In mingled shades of dark, reliev'd with green.

IX.

With nice research, how pleasing to unfold,
　The forms of matter which compose this earth :
In these the great omniscient cause behold—
　Of light, of motion, and prolific birth.

X.

But who can speak of power which knows no bound?—
　From the tall trees, whose branches wide expand,
To the fair flowers, like smiling gems around,
　We trace the wonders of the master's hand.

XI.

Admire him, in that orb, whose potent beam
　Now gladdens, vivifies, and brightens all ;
Behold him, in that gentle, fostering stream,
　Sent on the grass and springing herbs to fall.

XII.

His bounty gave yon herds, which graze the field,—
 The flocks, which yield our country's pride, the fleece,
For man's sole use, with all which earth can yield,—
 Would man but share these ample gifts in peace!

XIII.

Then how can we, presumptuous, thoughtless, vain,
 Forget that God who all these blessings gave ;—
Harden'd by pride, His holy laws disdain,
 Who freely pardons all who truly crave.

XIV.

He, who for sin, the precious ransom paid,
 Is ever near, though pain and gloom surround :
Safe may we walk where treacherous snares are laid,
 Through Him, in whom all love, all joy, is found.

XV.

How poor are earth's rewards compar'd to this!
 Ensnaring wealth, and glory's phantom show :—
Then let us not forego undying bliss,
 To taste of springs which but a moment flow.

XVI.

Whilst here we muse on wonders, let us raise
    Thanksgiving to the all-sustaining power;
For on the humblest, who devoutly praise,
    Will nurturing love, and grace enduring shower.

ON THE OBSERVATORY

AT MONK-BRETTON, NEAR BARNSLEY.

I.

FAIR tower! that braves the flying storm,
  When vengeance arms its wing;
I mark thy bold, commanding form,
  While thoughts spontaneous spring.
How sweet! from thy wind-shaken brow,
To gaze on all, which thou canst show,
  Where charms so richly blend.
Towns, mansions, far around, are seen,
And through dark woods and meadows green,
  Smooth glancing waters bend.

II.

Here may the child of leisure stand
  To spend a pleasant hour;
And see far o'er this smiling land
  Each steeple, hall, and tower;—

The hills which form the prospect's bound,
The fertile plains and valleys, crown'd
  With herbage, fruit, and grain ;
And mark the bustling race of man,
Pursuing each his chosen plan,
  A hopeful end to gain.

III.

Lo! o'er Dearne's stream, that gently glides,
  Bleak Barnsley's cloud-wreath'd head ;
Where trade, not kind to all, provides
  Her children's well-earn'd bread.
Beyond the grounds of Stainbro' bloom,
Where Strafford rul'd—o'er whose dark doom
  A monarch's tears were shed.
O'er hills grove-tufted, seen to rise
Gay Wakefield's spire assails the skies ;
  Now, Beaumont's woodlands spread.

IV.

Here, Hickleton's exalted pile,
  There, Wharncliffe's borders view :
Dear Wentworth's beauties yonder smile,
  In Summer's liveliest hue.

Should optic power assist the sight,
The eye may speed its joyful flight,
 Where nobler scenes expand—
See Ebor's sacred splendour smile—
With awe regard that mighty pile !—
 The glory of our land.

V.

Thou* lifts thy head above the plain,
 In monumental pride,
Like landmark, seen from stormy main,
 The seaman's course to guide :
Or, like some friendly beacon's form,
Uprear'd to warn against the storm,
 When war's mad horrors gloom :
As when Napoleon awed the world,
Ere his vast hopes were prostrate hurl'd,
 By dread relentless doom.

VI.

Art thou a calm retreat, design'd
 For wisdom's studious race ?

---

* The Observatory.

From whence the truth-delighting mind,
   May soar in boundless space—
On each revolving planet gaze—
The polar star, the comet's blaze—
   Orion's brilliant glance—
And every constellation bright,
Which, gleaming through the veil of night,
   Illumes the wide expanse.

VII.

If vers'd in astronomic lore
   I could the tube apply ;
With Herschell's spirit, to explore
   The orb-illumin'd sky—
Or science in fair walks pursue,
Which heaven-bless'd Newton laid to view,
   I glad with thee would stay—
So, beaming from thy stately brow,
O'er this dark region long might glow
   The light of learning's ray.

ON ARRIVING AT MANHOOD.

I.

Tʜɪs day shall not unhonour'd fly,
What others do, one can but try,
   A birth-day carol sing!
Not to proclaim the noble birth
Of one ordain'd to shine on earth,
   A statesman, peer, or king;—

II.

Nor yet a warrior or divine;
I would not stoop to grace the shrine
   Of pride, with fulsome strain;
I simply would commemorate,
A youth arriv'd at man's estate,
   Myself a humble swain.

IX.

For years the muse's chorded shell,
Like Chrysalis in dormant cell,
  With me in torpor lay;
Now, reconcil'd to scenes of strife,
An insect, fluttering into life.
  I sport in transient day.

X.

To day, I'm what is call'd of age,
Thus far advanc'd upon my stage,
  Yet form'd no final plan:
Th' apostle said,—When fully grown,
He left all childish acts alone,—
  In word and deed a man.

XI.

Few tread his manly, righteous way;
By all who preach, and all who pray,
  His love is not possess'd;
In garb of sanctity array'd,
How many by their deeds have made
  Religion but a jest.

XII.

I, luckless wight, scarce fit for this,
Or, for a sphere of perfect bliss,
  With dark presage begin;
But shall I change? as change I may,
Or blindly keep the beaten way,
  Of smooth alluring sin?

XIII.

The last most like—by syrens led,
(Though treacherous,) soft, and fair to tread,
  Is pleasure's soothing glade;
Too late, sincerely I may mourn,
That, by wild passions onward borne,
  In error's path I stray'd.

XIV.

Ah me! that youth should madly choose,
Like wanton courser, bounding loose,
  To chase where pleasure flies;
How much unlike Alcides' choice,
Who, charm'd by modest virtue's voice,
  Pursued a nobler prize.

I

XV.

Upgrown, how few from evil turn!
The checks of conscience still they spurn,
   And warnings are forgot ;
Vice triumphs, spite of preachers' pains,
The rogue, the hypocrite remains,
   The reprobate, and sot.

XVI.

The love of mirth, of wit, and wine,
This last, (thank Heaven,) no fault of mine,
   And love of wealth and fame,
Are each indulg'd by man and youth,
While virtue, honesty, and truth,
   Can few staunch votaries claim.

XVII.

But why should I, unskill'd, unwise,
On others harshly moralize,
   And not myself restrain ;
That valued maxim—" Know Thyself,"
Too oft is laid upon the shelf,
   By busy meddlers vain.

XVIII.

And do I know myself? ah! no,
As feelings prompt, I forward go,
   Unconscious where I tend;
While some on me with wonder glance,
Or scorn which blends with ignorance;—
   And kindly some befriend:

XIX.

Shall I yet twang my trembling harp,
While self-elected critics carp,
   And fools their verdict pass;
While generous censors are but few,
Whose truly just and sound review,
   Might prove a faithful glass.

XX.

Upon the world my verse to throw,
Already fill'd to overflow,
   Appears indeed unwise:
Though tempted by the love of gain,
Or, throbbing, eager to obtain
   Fame's more unstable prize.

XXI.

For wealth, can short-liv'd man implore?—
A guard from penury, at my door
   Would amply serve for me:
I scorn the grovelling hireling band,
Who, for their trifling toils, demand
   So undeserv'd a fee.

XXII.

To please my friends or soothe my breast,
I'll sing when fancy prompts me best,
   As truth and reason guide—
Since Heaven hath powers bestow'd on man,
To aid the universal plan,
   Those powers should be applied.

XXIII.

For in this world of care and grief,
Good deeds will yield the best relief
   The darkest moments cheer,
And thus the feeble powers I boast,
Should not in wasteful sloth be lost,
   But virtuous toil revere.

XXIV.

My actions, time alone will tell,
If I employ my talent well,
  The good will rest with me ;
And now, O muse, if gifted, say
Before another natal day
  What shall my portion be ?

XXV.

Shall I be seeking, void of skill,
For peace, in gloom and error still,
  Or, by sweet mercy's aid,—
Be rid of future doubts and fears,—
Or mov'd from this dark vale of tears
  In earth's cold bosom laid.

XXVI.

How futile is the wish to know,
What none of mortal mould can show—
  'Events of future day !
Now spurning vain desires from me—
Resign'd to Heaven's supreme decree,
  I end my wandering lay.

IN MEMORY OF DR. CHAS. OXLEY

(LATE OF PONTEFRACT.)

THOUGH death with keen unerring dart,
Despising all the powers of art,
Hath cut, so soon, the vital chord
Of one who long will be deplor'd ;
In whose superior, cultur'd mind,
Were wisdom's noblest stores combin'd:
Though he from earthly sphere has rent,
A life in useful service spent ;
By whose severe untimely doom,
The brightest hopes are sunk in gloom,
The fairest prospect is—a tomb:
Though he has quench'd the purest flame,
That ever breath'd in mortal frame ;
And though the blow from us doth sever
A heart that will be cherish'd ever ;—
This consolation cheers us still,
The ransom'd soul he cannot kill:

Which, pregnant with celestial breath,
Defies the rigid grasp of death,—
Leaves far behind the cheerless night,
To breathe in realms of purest light;—
Ascends, exulting, from the sod,
To worship at the throne of God.
That such may be the glorious meed,
Of Him whom Heaven hath doom'd to bleed;
Inspir'd by faith, we firmly trust,
While weeping o'er his sacred dust.

A PRAYER.

I.

Thou Power ador'd ! whom all may find,
 That seek in truth thy way;
Who art to all thy creatures kind,
 Though far from thee we stray;—

II.

Thou seest thy trembling suppliant bow,
 Thou hear'st his lowly prayer;
Preserve me from my treacherous foe,
 And burst his cruel snare.

III.

Thy love, so radiant, yet so mild,
 Illum'd my darkest hour;
For e'en upon a wayward child
 Thy blessings freely pour.

IV.

Before my eyes, in full design,
  That path of mercy lay,
Which leads to where thy glories shine,
  Yet strait and rude the way.

V.

Though conscious of thy presence here,
  And lighted by thy smile,
Yet oft the rebel, lurking near,
  Will my weak heart beguile.

VI.

But Thou, whose voice controuls the wind,
  And stills the maddening sea,
My fierce conflicting powers canst bind,
  Subservient all to thee.

VII.

Once more, in mercy, stretch thine arm—
  Restrain the lawless tide,
Of passions flowing high and warm,
  Which none but Heaven can guide.

VIII.

Teach me, in every state, to know
   Thy precepts, and revere;
Since all I have to thee I owe,
   Move in my soul thy fear.

IX.

Grant me that meek, submissive frame,
   When I can truly say,
I seek not joy, I ask not fame,
   To smile, 'til time decay.

X.

Not lur'd by folly's idle dream,
   Nor honour's cheating show :—
Lord, bow me to thy will supreme,
   Who all my wants must know.

XI.

Though oft above our path of woes,
   Clouds frown in dark array;
Their gloom, how light ! if, at the close,
   Thy beams celestial play.

XII.

When life's last faintly-heaving breath,
  From its frail home is flown,
Through Him, who lov'd us unto death—
  O make me then thy own.

THE EMIGRANT MOTHER TO HER FIRST-BORN.*

I.

First-fruit of those who love thee,
　Lone floweret of the wild !
Whose little features prove thee
　My own—my precious child.

II.

How warms thy mother's bosom,
　While thee her arms caress ;
Thou tender, opening blossom,
　That charm'st the wilderness.

---

* The female emigrant whose departure from England is mentioned in the poem at page 73, is married to a brother of the author's. This child of the woods, whose birth will make the Canadian solitudes more pleasant and endurable, is the offspring of their faithful affection.

III.

Kind Heaven in love provided,
   And gave this cherish'd dower,
When from all else divided,
   To cheer my lonely hour.

IV.

For while thy sire is bending
   In duty's arduous field,
Thy voice thy smiles sweet blending,
   A grateful solace yield.

V.

For him the rude sea daring,
   I left my home behind ;
Dear social ties all tearing,—
   Here more than home I find.

VI.

His arm the strong axe wielding,
   Hath laid the forest low,
And rais'd this kind roof, shielding
   From raving storm and snow.

VII.

And now, while vernal pleasure
  And beauty, cheer our land,
The future harvest-treasure
  Is scatter'd from his hand.

VIII.

'T is our's his toil to lighten,
  In deepest cares to please,—
His harass'd looks to brighten,
  At eve's kind hour of ease.

IX.

Fair o'er yon forest bowers
  The last mild sunbeams stay;
And rich from breathing flowers
  The vesper breezes play.

X.

To our lone cot retiring,
  His meal will we prepare;
For lo! new joy inspiring—
  He comes to bless us there.

XI.

Though painful tasks achieving,
  No murmur leaves his breast;
Content, a balm relieving,
  Bids aching trouble rest.

XII.

Dear hope—her aid bestowing,
  Sees now a brighter day,
When streams of plenty flowing,
  Will here in gladness play.

XIII.

Lo! rugged Nature, bending,
  To nerves unshrinking, yields;
And forests dark ascending,
  Give place to smiling fields.

XIV.

And oh, forgive, just Heaven,
  A pleading mother's love;
To thee, sweet babe, be given
  These better days to prove!

XV.

That Power—o'er earth so spacious,
 Who rules, in town, or wild—
Even here, all good—all gracious,
 Will care for thee, my child!

XVI.

His bounty free will nourish—
 Our fondest labours aid;
And bid our offspring flourish,
 When low our heads are laid.

Lightning Source UK Ltd.
Milton Keynes UK
UKHW020030051021
391660UK00007B/1597